SIX WEEKS IN AFRICA

by

Grahame Elson

Published by Grahame Elson

9781983132469

To Shaun,

Without whose patience and encouragement none of this would
have been possible.

Get in touch;

Sixweekstravel@gmail.com

Twitter @GrahameElson

FOREWARD

If we have some money spare and have a choice between, let us say, home improvements or a holiday then we are obviously going to book a holiday. Who the hell wouldn't! Nobody on their deathbed ever thanked God for the new carpet in the spare room.

Of course, it's not just the holiday that's enjoyable, it's also the anticipation beforehand. Whenever things seem a little bit shit you can always say 'only x number of weeks till I fly'. I did just that when I discovered that I'm now so overweight I need to hold my breath to tie my shoelaces!

What follows is just a sample of the travelling we have done over the years focused, as the title suggests, on the time we spent in Africa.

All I hope for is that you enjoy reading about our adventures and that maybe it will inspire you on your next holiday to throw down your book at the poolside and go out to see something instead.

EGYPT

Myself and my partner Shaun were lucky enough to visit Egypt three times between 2001 and 2008 well before the Arab Spring, military coups and global terror networks came together to make it an altogether more hazardous and unlikely place to holiday. We cruised down the Nile from Luxor to Aswan, visited the bustling metropolis of Cairo and experienced the Red Sea coast at both Hurghada and Sharm El Sheikh.

Our first time in Egypt was also my first time in Africa and my first foreign holiday with my other half and I was picturing us in white cotton shirts and Panama hats, sipping G&T's on the deck of our Nile cruise ship before disembarking at ancient yet stunning locations in the great and empty stretches along the banks of the Nile. This illusion was quickly shattered by Luxor airport where my naiveté about foreign travel became all too apparent. This place was a shit hole!

If there is a dirtier, noisier and more badly organised airport in the world then I have yet to find it and my mood was not improved at baggage collection where I found my suitcase had a large and well defined muddy footprint right in the middle. A muddy footprint I might add which proved responsible for my new sunglasses being smashed beyond repair.

First though we had to navigate passport control where we were required to have the appropriate visa's, immigration paperwork, customs declarations and camcorder permissions. I believe that this will be simpler after BREXIT when we will simply have to say,

"British, less of your nonsense" and walk straight through. We then found our travel rep who told us where to get our transfer and it at last seemed possible to relax a little and at this point a very helpful young man approached me and enquired of me with a single spoken word,

"Thomson?" while indicating that he was here to carry my luggage.

"Why yes." came my impressed reply as they were indeed my travel company and I, without hesitation, handed over my luggage. My mood worsened further as negotiations on his fee to hand my luggage back began in earnest once we had reached the coach.

So, this place wasn't what I had expected it to be, but as it turns out that's the best part of travelling. Here I was in Egypt, Land of the Pharaohs, home to the Pyramids, the Sphinx, the valleys of the Kings, Antiquities beyond counting and the Nile. Egypt is a million square kilometres in size which is four times larger than the U.K. and is almost entirely arid, sparsely populated desert (The Arabian desert to the east and the Libyan desert to the west). Virtually everyone lives on a single green strip a few miles either side of the Nile as it dissects the country from North to South. Although most people including myself associate the Nile with Egypt it is the most dominant geographical features of North-East Africa with the Nile basin taking in not only Egypt but also Uganda, Kenya, The Congo, Sudan and Ethiopia. The rainfall across this vast area trickles down, joining together forming streams and tributaries, growing in strength and forming the longest river in the world at over four thousand miles in length. The shortest river in comparison is the D river is the U.S. at just 37 metres in case you're interested! Its journey from the Egyptian/Sudanese border up to where it meets the Mediterranean is simply the concluding part of its journey and we would spend the first week sailing along only a small fraction of that final part between Luxor and Aswan. Here it is easily navigable and there is an astounding concentration of destinations for intrepid travellers like ourselves to visit.

The Nile has of course played a pivotal role in the development of the country as it has defined the environment over millennia but into that environment came people and their activities can be traced back more than a hundred thousand years as evidenced by the stone implements uncovered at numerous archaeological digs. The excavation of well-preserved Tombs has given archaeologists a wealth of information about the history some six thousand years ago and if you jump forward to three or four thousand years ago we have the monuments for which the country is perhaps most famous with their inscriptions, carvings and pictures which record many of the great and not so great events. Egypt was a power in the known world with a wealthy society for some and a complex set of religious beliefs which resulted in the construction of the mighty temples which millions of people, including us, have visited. Their history has been preserved, buried in the sands of the desert, protected from the passage of time until they were unearthed, restored and preserved by a colossal effort of the Egyptian people with some international support.

From Tutankhamen to Cleopatra and on to Nasser, from ancient wonders such as the Pyramids through to the Suez Canal and the Aswan Dam it has been important. Muslim invaders, Roman invaders, British and French invaders and a starring role in the Cold War struggle between the Americans and the Russians to name just a few has seen Egypt in the centre of the action both diplomatically and militarily for over a millennia. Britain's own fortunes have been tied to events here for more than two centuries from Horatio Nelson's victory over the French fleet in the Nile which secured our supply lines to India and established us as a World Power to Field Marshall Montgomery's defeat of the Nazi forces at El Alamein, the first real victory for the Allies in the Second World War and the point at which the tide began to turn, and finally to the humiliation of the Suez crisis which perhaps more than any other event exposed Britain's Imperial pretensions as so much hot air.

As I sat on that coach heading to our river cruise ship, The Commodore, I stared out of the window trying to take everything in. Everything appeared to be half finished, every house missing a roof or a wall, every pavement a death trap with loose stones and every road surface making you thankful for modern suspension. We saw a set of road works where a deep pit had been dug right through the road and pavement around which there were no warning signs or barriers. To allow the traffic to pass they had slung some sheets of metal over the hole which buckled and bent alarmingly with the passing of the traffic but no one seemed to care. Ad hoc stalls along the roadside were offering a positive cornucopia of products for sale including food being prepared right next to groups of goats, cows and donkeys who were shitting extravagantly on every available surface. To top it all off as we neared our destination we passed an irrigation channel which was supposed to carry inland the life-giving waters of the river to the crops in the fields. The life-giving water in this case was a luminous shade of green with the bloated corpse of a donkey floating in it. There was just a glimmer of concern that raised itself at the back of my mind wondering what we had let ourselves in for but before the thought could fester we arrived at the dock and were greeted by our travel rep, a pleasant lady whom I shall call Sarah with long frizzy ginger hair and a complexion that could not have been less suited to such a sunny environment. She had been escorting this particular holiday for many years she explained but her job was simply to deal with every gripe and complaint that a hundred British tourists can think of during a week on holiday, for the excursions we would have a dedicated Egyptian guide. As we chatted with her and discussed our journey from the airport she told us that its most unusual to see a dead animal abandoned like the poor donkey in the irrigation channel as livestock is the most expensive asset that families here have and after death it is still of use for its meat and hide and any bits left over may be sold on to the local zoo to feed the big cats! In case you doubt my word about the importance of animals here let me tell you about a tragedy which occurred in a small village called Nazlat Imara. One of the families who lived there had many animals on which they relied including a flock of chickens. One day the 18-year-old son saw one of these chickens fall into the well from where their water was drawn and without hesitation he followed it down into the darkness in an attempt to rescue it. Concerned for his welfare he was followed by his sister and two brothers who according to police weren't even able to swim and then to finish off two elderly farmers who had witnessed the commotion also headed down into the well as well, if you see what I mean. They all drowned and it was left to the police to pull their bodies back out some days later. They also pulled out the chicken. It survived!

Anyway, we were to be on the cruise for a week, starting and finishing in Luxor we would be visiting Luxor temple, Karnak, the Valley of the Kings, Kom Ombo, Philae, Esna Locks, Edfu, Abu Simbel, Aswan and the Aswan Dam, Dendera and a lot more. Its bloody good value and quite some going to get that lot in during just one week. A lot of the sailing would be done overnight so each morning we would be in a new location and ready to be whisked off for a sightseeing tour. We were very fortunate with the room that we were allocated as we were a good distance from the noisy engine room and very close to the restaurant and most important of all, we had a window on the starboard side. All of the cruise ships that sail the Nile will dock next to each other at night so you have to walk through several other ships to get to the shore. To our great good fortune the Commodore was always the last ship to dock and being on the starboard side meant that we always had a stunning view of the river and the opposite bank to wake up to each morning. For the majority on board the only view you can look forward to is the window of someone's cabin on the next ship over. I suppose if you're lucky this could deliver a few thrilling sights as well but probably not Egypt related ones.

The Nile Commodore was sat waiting for us. We walked up the red carpeted gang plank and entered into a world that was everything I could have hoped for, wood panels, plush carpets and a décor that put me in mind of the 1930's, although perhaps a little faded. My image of us sipping G&T's would be right at home here although it would be minus the Panama Hat as I had discovered that wearing one made me look like a complete tit. The overall effect of the boat was somewhat tarnished by the machine guns mounted around the perimeters and the armed undercover officers who were to be found patrolling the hallways. They were very friendly though as were all the staff, striving to be helpful, attentive and yet still unobtrusive. On checking in reception informed us that no tips would be expected during our stay but that at the end of our holiday a single tip could be left to share amongst all the crew including the engineers, kitchen staff and assorted other people who you never see but who are still vital to your holiday. The ship was to be an oasis of calm and the only place on our holiday where we would not be constantly hassled to part with our money. We surrendered our passports and were taken to our room which was splendid. It was spacious (by no means certain when on a cruise), well-furnished and had a substantially sized window from which to enjoy the passing scenery. There were two sets of curtains, a normal patterned set on the interior and a second thicker set behind which could have doubled up as the cladding on a nuclear reactor. The sun is very intense and the heat that would radiate through a normal set of curtains would quickly make the room unbearable, the lead shielding curtains would at least keep the temperature within human tolerance.

We unpacked, quickly filling the six available coat hangers which for some reason all hotels consider adequate for two people, and then set off to explore the boat. Standing four floors high above the water line the first two decks were filled with the passenger's rooms, engineering, kitchens and assorted other places we either didn't want to go to or weren't allowed to go. The third deck, on which our room was found, contained the bridge, more rooms for passengers and the dining room and then the top deck contained the bar, outside seating areas and the plunge pool. There was an outside seating area at the front where you could sit and see where we were headed, then the bar with dance floor, card table and television viewing area, followed by a canvas covered seating area and then finally the plunge pool surrounded by the sun loungers for those who wished to dramatically increase their chances of getting skin cancer. I would not be counted amongst their number having stocked up on long sleeved shirts, a wide brimmed hat in Sri Lankan style (in which I did not look a complete tit) and factor 50 sun cream. My freckles and pale skin meant that I was as ill-suited to this environment as our travel rep and it ensures that instead of tanning I go bright red and then all my skin falls off which is both unpleasant for me to experience and for other people to look at. It feels as though someone should be walking five paces in front of me ringing a bell and shouting "unclean, unclean!"

We didn't sail that first night as a trip to Luxor temple was planned for the early hours of the following morning and that's where we shall go next.

In the early hours of the following day and with the world outside still shrouded in darkness it was actually a little chilly as we stepped outside and my clothing choice of a thin t-shirt with shorts suddenly seemed questionable but there was no time to head back and change. Our holiday rep Sarah was already stood at the bottom of the gang plank surrounded on all sides by ratty passengers who had clearly not anticipated rising at such a refreshing hour of the day. She remained resolutely cheerful in spite of this and busied herself organising the group for the trip and simultaneously smoothing over the assorted grievances about room locations, hot drinks selections and the temperature of the boat which several of our fellow passengers felt could not wait and needed to be raised right this very second. Arseholes!

As each of us approached she would consult her clipboard and point us in the direction of one of two coaches. The coach on which you found yourself would determine if you were to be a 'cougar' or a 'panther'. A chap called David was waiting for us at our coach and introduced himself to us with a firm handshake. In his late 30's, southern Egyptian, smartly turned out and very well spoken he had a definite sense of authority about him. The authority was a very good thing for him as it meant he could lie to us convincingly whenever we asked a question that he didn't know the answer to!

The coach once fully loaded departed from the dock and began its journey through the relatively empty streets of Luxor and David now rose at the front of the coach, microphone in hand and began dishing out instructions and itineraries to ensure that our tour ran with clockwork precision. We were shown his hat which would be held up into the air at any point of interest. The raising of the hat was the signal that wisdom was about to be imparted. He checked we all had our water and plenty of sun cream and finally he informed us that henceforth we would be know collectively as the 'panthers' which he was a lot more excited about than seemed justified.

So here we were in Luxor, the ancient capital city formerly known as Thebes. There are six great temples here, on the right bank of the river stands Karnak and Luxor, the famous ones that any visitor to Egypt is going to get taken to along with four more on the left bank called Goornah, Medinet Habu, The Ramesseum and Deir-el-Bahri which are the ones that won't be included in your holiday and require an optional excursion. We would be lucky to take in a thousandth of what was on offer, although it's probably the best thousandth when you think about it so it probably doesn't matter too much.

"If you could all walk up this street and turn right at McDonalds you can then wait by the ticket booth" David shouted holding up his hat.

Welcome to the mystery and wonder of ancient Egypt I thought as we passed by Maccie D's but we were to find throughout our time here that there is a mixture of the oddly familiar and exotically different. Fast food restaurants like McDonalds and Pizza Hut with their fixed price menus vied with locally owned restaurants serving local delicacies where every price was open to barter. Horse drawn carriages called Kaleshes shared the roads with Vauxhall Corsas and we found the Zebra crossings which are familiar were also different as none of the drivers here would ever dream of stopping or even slowing down for them.

We were stood a little way up from the front entrance of the temple and were gazing up at the toweringly high walls some 75 feet tall that should have been fronted by two Obelisks. There is now only one Obelisk that rises even higher than the great stone walls behind it. The other now stands in the middle of the Place de la Concorde in Paris. They are made from yellow granite and are covered in hieroglyphs which celebrate the rule of Ramses II. The one in Paris was given as a gift to the French back in 1829 by the self-proclaimed ruler of Egypt Muhammed Ali Pasha but it took the French three years to overcome the enormous technical difficulties of moving it and several more years until it was finally mounted in the centre of their Capital City. If you should care to visit Paris and take a look you will find the pedestal on which it now stands has a series of drawings on it that depict the complex machinery that was used to overcome the difficulties of transporting and erecting the Obelisk there all those years ago. For that extra bit of 'wow' factor it is now topped by a gold leafed pyramid cap to replace the one that was stolen over a thousand years ago by tomb raiders. The French were offered the other obelisk as a gift as well but graciously declined as the feat of moving 250 tons of granite without breaking it was so expensive and complicated they figured that the one they had would probably be enough. At least that means the Egyptian people still have one of them to look at.

The French Obelisk now stands where the guillotine used to be during the French Revolution, possibly the most potent symbol of that time of terror, so I think we can safely say that it is somewhat of an improvement from an aesthetic point of view if a little less exciting with regard to the blood and gore side of things.

The Temple at Luxor was constructed in 1400 B.C. and has spent most of its life since then abandoned and buried under sand, eventually being covered over by the streets and houses of Luxor city until its importance was realised and excavation work started in the 1880's. It took decades for the painstaking recovery of the site and the work was not completed until the 1960's. This is not surprising as removing all the modern infrastructure and then the accumulated waste of the centuries without causing any damage to the structure of the temple is a task fit for Hercules. Imagine how much work is involved and how much money would have to be spent simply to compensate and move the resident population out before you can even start digging. There is even a Mosque called the Abu Haggag which still remains and which as a holy site had to be persevered, this is now about ten metres up in the air as the ground around it was dug out to reveal all of the ancient stonework underneath. We spent several hours touring the site and being talked through a seemingly never-ending history which led to a critical information overload in my brain. The history is so varied from speculation over construction techniques to the stories of the ancient Egyptians onto Roman occupation and up to European colonial wars. The temple is regarded as one of the greatest monuments of Thebes and has been described as the largest open-air museum in the world, standing close to the river bank and measuring some 250 metres in length. It was built by Amenhotep III to honour the triad gods of Amen, Mut and Khansu. It was also hastily completed and should have been considerably larger with plans for a large hypostyle hall like that at Karnak which were abandoned with only the colonnade completed. The construction of this one temple bares the imprint of Amenhotep III and IV, Rameses II, Tutankhamen, Horemheb as well as Alexander the Great who was here and who rebuilt the sanctuary area.

We were enthralled and spent a diverting morning looking at statues, chapels, obelisks, sphinxes, murals and colonnades as well as some graffiti left by both British and French troops during their respective occupations of the area. This mostly consisted of them carving their name and regiment into the stone work of the temple, a 19th century equivalent of 'Jonny woz ere'. This was followed up by a visit to a small surviving area of the avenue of the sphinxes, a grand avenue that originally lead from Luxor temple to Karnak temple. Unfortunately much of it has been destroyed, mostly by the Romans who built roads and houses over the top and smashed up the sphinxes to provide the building material. At its height the avenue was 70 metres wide and had more than a thousand sphinxes lining it. Restoration projects have been running on the site to try and repair some of the damage as well as removing the modern housing that has covered so much of it even until quite recently. In spite of this lack of care over the centuries it is still a site much worth visiting and it at least gives you a flavour of what was once here. If you ever get the chance to visit please don't be the sort of tourist who leaves reviews like this on trip advisor;

"Went to visit the temple - quite disappointed. You can pretty much see everything from the fence so didn't waste our money". It takes a special sort of ability to visit somewhere like this and take away that, and I think it underlines an important point that some people are just dicks.

After a thoroughly diverting morning the time to head back to the coach arrived and we had to return to the Commodore. The temperature had been steadily rising through the morning and we were beginning to appreciate the universal instruction for all tours in Egypt, bring water! We had both invested in a cooler bag for our chilled water bottles and this had turned out to be an entirely useless investment as after several hours out and about in the sunshine the water was hot enough to make a passable cup of tea. The only useful feature was the shoulder strap that at least made carrying the bottle around a bit easier bit sipping warm water does nothing to properly quench your thirst and we were both ready for a very large and preferably very fizzy drink.

We arrived back at the ship and after a quick shower to remove the layers of dried sweat and dirt that we had acquired during the morning we dressed for breakfast. Dressed is perhaps overstating it a little but the rules on board forbade the wearing of shorts in the dining room and so I opted to go the full Marks & Spencer's with a pair of cream chinos and a white linen shirt.

Breakfast abroad is always a slightly disappointing affair with the usual pretend 'full English' with limp bacon, those horrible sausages which seem to be mostly meat (unlike a good old British Sausage which is mostly something else!), undercooked scrambled egg, something approximating to tea and the promise of fresh fruit juice which is all too often a cordial that has been diluted to within an inch of its life. The cereal was not much better and I was horrified to discover as I tucked into my first spoonful that the milk was warm. Surely there had been some sort of mistake, the idea of cornflakes without ice cold milk was an abomination to my mind but there was no mistake, the milk would always be served warm and the most I could hope for was that it was fresh and from a cow. Lunch and dinner were an entirely different affair with a huge selection of delicious meals on offer and there wasn't a day where we couldn't find something to tantalise our taste buds. Sumptuous portions of creamy mashed potatoes or gorgeously plump and golden chips, seasonable vegetables of many types all cooked to perfection or a side salad with choices of fish, chicken and red meats in a dizzying array of combinations. All of this would be washed down with a plentiful amount of wine and finished off with puddings that had me within 3 calories of diabetes by the end of the week.

The ship would now spend the rest of the day and most of the night sailing to our next destination which would be Edfu where we would visit the temple of Horus and then onto the temple of Kom Ombu. For now we could relax on board the ship, watch the world drift by and play with the video camera that I had borrowed from my parents but didn't know how to use. As we sat up on the deck we saw in the distance the Esna Lock. The Nile at this point is straddled by two barrage bridges, one of which was built by the British over a 100 years ago and the second an electricity generation bridge constructed in the 1990's by the Egyptian authorities. These bridges cause a large difference in the level of the Nile and all the ships wishing to pass through this area have to pass through the Esna Lock and this can lead to delays of several hours or possibly days if you are particularly unlucky. Never seemingly able to miss a sales opportunity some hardy retailers will row out to the ship while you're waiting and attempt to sell you an assortment of fabrics and souvenirs from their little boats. This is done by holding a position just off the side of the ship and shouting up at the tourists on the top deck. Once they have your attention they will begin throwing the merchandise up to you sealed in a plastic bag or possibly not, you can then inspect the goods and if you want them you enter into a shouting match with the seller to negotiate a mutually acceptable price. We were advised that It was a good idea to use the little plastic cases that camera films come in to throw any money back down to the traders, that way if you missed it would at least float long enough for them to get to it. Quite what will be used in this new digital age when people don't have camera film anymore I don't know. We sat back and half watched this ad hoc market take place with the rest of my attention focused on the video camera. This was not a modern piece of equipment being about the size of a small car and requiring the use of a video cassette (ask your parents). On returning home we would find that fully half of the video footage taken would consist of watching the lock gates open and then close again and was a contender for the most boring film in history except for The Holiday starring Jude Law of course. We did find when we were over in Sharm el Sheik a few year later that Russian tourists were the masters of the boring holiday video. The hotel we had booked had a majority of Russian guests, all couples and all the men were large intimidating looking types with special forces tattoos accompanied by their mostly petite and scantily clad partners. Their idea of capturing holiday memories was for the women to lounge around in unlikely locations in various states of undress while the husband filmed them from all sides. When I say unlikely locations I mean in the middle of flowerbeds, lying on the paths, leaning at the bar, or propped up against the rear walls of the hotel by the bins. It never seemed to occur to them to film the view. It was all just close-ups of the women in random locations. The only other notable feature of the Russians was that they were the only guests at the hotel who were not allowed to take glasses away from the bar. The management had reserved the right to only serve them in plastic cups and when you enquired of any of the staff as to why this was the case they would lower their voice, look from side to side in a conspiratorial manor and simply say that there had been an 'incident' about which they could speak no more! I never did get to the bottom of it.

The next day we were again awoken at an impossibly early hour so we could visit the temple at Edfu first which is remarkably complete. This is a temple built of sandstone and the imposing outer walls completely dominate the surrounding town. This temple like Luxor was built over many generations with different sections being added over time. The central building was begun by Ptolemy III in 237 B.C. and took 25 years to complete. Completion of the outer walls and decorations took until 57 B.C. being completed under Ptolemy XII which is a staggering length of time for the construction of just one project, although I believe the third runway at Heathrow may well run it a close second by the time it's done. The temple of Horus as it should be properly named is the second largest temple in Egypt after Karnak and it is very well preserved. It was constructed much later than most of the other temples that have survived but was again buried in sand and built over thus offering it some protection from the passage of time and the inscriptions on its walls have been an important source of information regarding construction techniques as well as explanations of the myths and religion of the Greco-Roman period in Egypt.

The site is dedicated to the falcon god Horus and contains a large pillared hall with two smaller halls adjoined and a sanctuary surrounded by chapels where the business of deity worship could be properly undertaken. Horus was a man with the head of a falcon and was usually depicted wearing a red and white crown which signified his kingship over the entire kingdom, the first truly national god although according to the mythology this wasn't always the case. His role was as the god of war, of hunting and of the sky and his eyes were believed to be the sun and the moon so when you saw them passing across the sky you were looking at the god himself passing over you. Now you would think that as they are both his eyes they would look the same but one of his eyes was gouged out during a great and vicious battle with another god called Set and had to be replaced for him by the moon god Khonsu, thus explaining the altered appearance. Before I recount the story of the conflict between Horus and Set its important to point out that there are almost as many variations of this story as there are people to ask about it. There are many contradictions, sometimes in the telling of a single version. Horus and Set may have been brothers or they may have been Uncle and Nephew, in my telling of the conflict Horus and Set will be our protagonists although it's easy to find other versions of the story where their mother/uncle/other gods are held to be responsible for some of the actions described, this is no more than my best understanding of the story after hearing three or four different versions of it.

Set was the god of the north, or the god of the red lands, or at least of the desert. Horus was the god of the south, or the plains or of the black soil. Set killed Horus's father and was determined to destroy Horus also and claim the title of King God of all Egypt. Horus had other ideas. There battles were spoken of for their viciousness and lack of mercy and the situation became so grave that the other gods decided that they must step in to arbitrate and save any more bloodshed and mutilation. Horus may well have lost an eye which was bad for him but spare a thought for Set who had lost his testicles, according to the myth that is the reason that the deserts which he represented are now infertile. The gods set many challenges in which Horus always emerged as the winner even if it involved a little bit of cheating. When challenged to race stone boats down the Nile the stone boat crewed by Set immediately sank while the wooden boat that had been painted to look like stone by Horus won the race. The creator god who was judging preferred Set and always found a reason not to rule in Horus's favour resulting in the conflict dragging on for over 80 years. Eventually it was decided between the creator god and some other minor deities who were helping that a judgement would be passed based upon the semen of Horus and Set, semen being a very potent and powerful symbol in ancient Egypt sometimes akin to poison. This is the key event in determining who will be the ruler of all the land and Set sexually abuses Horus to establish his dominance and humiliate his foe which is quite impressive considering he earlier lost both of his testicles. He mounts him from behind but Horus keeps his wits about him and places his hand between his legs at the critical moment, catching the semen and when Set is distracted he casts the handful into the Nile. Horus takes a less confrontational approach and when alone nips round to Set's vegetable garden where he has a wank over the lettuces (I swear I'm not making this up!) so that Set will ingest his semen during his evening meal. And so it was the following day when the creator god spoke unto the semen to ask who should be the supreme god that Set's semen answered from the river and Horus's semen answered from Set's belly. Truly there was only one god king of all Egypt.

After a morning of stories along these lines and having reached the conclusion that the ancient peoples of this land were bat-shit crazy it was time to head back to the Commodore. En-route we found a very well organised market rowed along just one side of the street. There was a large white line painted down the centre of the road and numerous members of the Tourist Police on hand. The Tourist Police are a dedicated force who's sole job is to keep the tourists safe and to offer assistance where necessary. There were over half a million Tourist Police alongside half a million Regular Police in Egypt out of a population of 67 million, at least according to David and at least at that time, the official figures seem subject to a staggering amount of variation and interpretation. For comparison the U.K. had 62 million citizens and only 100,000 officers in total. You could fairly describe Egypt as a police state and no mistake. The white line in the centre of the road gave you a choice. If you wished to go back to the coach without being accosted then you walked to the left of the line. If you want to get some souvenirs and wish to be drawn into the haggling associated with this then you walked to the right of the line. The police were there to ensure that the traders never crossed this boundary and their will was enforced by throwing stones at any trader who did.

The second temple of the day was to be Kom Ombo. In Arabic the name of the site means hill of gold and this place was selected by Tuthmosis III for the construction of a temple in honour of the crocodile headed god, Sobek. The crocodile is a revered animal here, so much so that there are mummified remains stored in the adjacent catacombs. Aside from the crocodile theme this place also contains an engraving which is thought to be the first representation in history of surgical instruments. It is believed to show forceps, scissors, dilators and scalpels as well as medicine bottles which date from Roman times. Quite remarkable really that the instruments they developed all that time ago can still be found in a modern operating theatre. The medical theme continued as we viewed an engraving which outlined the ideal position for a woman to be in when giving birth. It had never occurred to me that this is something I would be learning about in an ancient temple in the middle of a holiday but apparently Egypt has a remarkable history when it comes to the development of medicines years ahead of their time. Although they couldn't perform invasive surgery (no anaesthetic, imagine the screaming you would do before you died of shock) but they would happily drill a hole into your jaw to relieve an abscess, they could fill a rotting tooth, set broken bones and sort out dislocations, treat burns with a herbal ointment and could stitch a wound to aid its healing. Many if not most of these things could have proved to be a death sentence anywhere else in the world at that time but not here and as a result you could potentially live into your mid 30's. Not to be sniffed at back then. As well as the treatments they also showed a remarkable level of equality for the time with the earliest female physician Merit Ptah who practiced medicine 5000 years ago.

Aside from the ancient history this was a place that I was looking forward to a great deal as this was the temple that in the 1978 film Death on the Nile was used to stand in for Karnak. Kom Ombo occupies a beautiful position slightly raised on a small hill looking down on to the Nile and the external scene of their arrival at Karnak was filmed here due to its stunning location. The actual temple now being in the middle of a city and not exuding the right ambience for the scene. The internal scenes were filmed back at the Hypostyle hall at the actual temple but to my mind those external shots are some of the most stunning of the film even if they are a lie. Please forgive me if I digress for a moment but the director of photography for the film was a guy called Jack Cardiff and in my opinion he is deserving of some acknowledgment. Within the industry he was credited with an appreciation for the use of light and colour that marked him out from his competition. In fact his knowledge of the use of light by artists in their paintings was the reason he got his job as camera operator at Denham studios in 1936. He worked in black and white films and then on colour films and was the camera operator on the very first Technicolor film shot in Britain called Wings of the Morning (1937). He also mastered the transition into the digital age and though he was also an accomplished director he was still much sought after by other directors for the camera and photography work on their films. He worked with Errol Flynn, Alfred Hitchcock, Humphrey Bogart, Charlton Heston, Kirk Douglas, Martin Scorsese, Lauren Bacall, Sophie Loren, Marlene Dietrich, Arnold Schwarzenegger and Sylvester Stallone too name just a few. He was the only photographer that Marilyn Monroe trusted to make her look beautiful. He travelled to the Congo during the filming of The African Queen (1951) to photograph Bogart and he said that while 'Bogie' didn't care much about how he looked in front of the camera you had to watch his toupee, if the light was wrong you could see the gauze that held it in place. Now that is attention to detail. He won two academy awards, was an Honorary Member of the Guild of British Camera Technicians, a Fellow of the British Film Institute and an O.B.E. in the Queen's millennial New Years Honours List. His two academy awards were won in 1947 and 2000 which holds two separate records for the longest hiatus between awards and the longest time between first and last awards. If you get the chance there is a documentary and a book about him and they are well worth a look. I'm afraid that while David did his best to talk about Egyptian history my attention was focused on taking in the glorious location. Sometimes the tour guides can't see the wood for the trees and I felt like the history of which pharaoh built what and where wasn't really adding anything to the day for me but it was enjoyable none the less. Several hours slipped by in what seemed like the blink of an eye and it was definitely time to head back to the ship for some rest and recuperation. My clothes needed changing, my body re-hydrating and my armpits de-odorising. We also needed to make a purchase as we were heading to the Captain's Cocktail Party that evening and it was requested that we all wear traditional Egyptian dress. This was clearly designed to generate sales for the on-board gift shop but it sounded like a laugh so we did it anyway.

The traditional clothing we were sold was called a galabeya and was sold with a white head scarf which we had to be shown how to tie. Made of fine cotton it is a long flowing garment that slips over your head and flows down around your legs. Slits on each side allowed easy access to your shorts pockets underneath. Ours were definitely not for everyday wear but were fancy with a lot of black and gold patterning around the collar and sleeves, these were to be our Sunday best and we were charged a criminally inflated price to reflect that. Pleased with our purchases we retired to our room to dress and stepped out to the party.

The turnout was good and when we arrived the bar was already buzzing with activity. Every passenger had made the effort to dress up with only two exceptions. One was a particularly miserable old bastard who had decided that he would look an idiot if he wore the galabeya and so refused, thus ensuring that he looked like an idiot and a miserable old bastard! He was only spared the undivided attention of us all by the other person who had opted out of the traditional dress. This was a rather exuberant gent in his 30's who had decided to come in a sparkly, sequined and slinky dress along with a rather large and rather sparkly crown and who was informing anyone who would listen that he was Queen Nefertiti. His wife's face defies adequate description but the phrase 'long suffering' springs to mind. In his defence though he managed the impossible as a hundred British people who had felt self-conscious about going out in their unfamiliar new togs all suddenly felt as though they were under-dressed for the occasion. All in all it was a good night although in hindsight we stayed much later than was sensible considering the early start that was expected of us the next day.

And suddenly it is the next day and that would see us arrive in Aswan which still remains one of my favourite places in all the world. The pace of life here feels sedate in comparison to Cairo. Elephantine Island sits out in the middle of the Nile and provides an inviting prospect alongside a plethora of smaller islands around which you can take a trip on a traditional wooden sailing boat called a felucca. These sail boats, all strikingly white in colour, can take up to twenty people at a time out on the river for a little sight seeing which we duly did. The comfortable boat provided a superb vantage point from which to take a good look at Aswan and its surroundings. Elephantine Island was the location of the original town that existed before the rise of Aswan city and for a long time marked the border between Egypt and the Nubian lands that were to be found to the south. Depending on who you talk to you may be told that the Islands original name was either 'yebu' or 'abu' but everyone agreed that this meant elephant and that it was derived from the smooth grey boulders that sit in the river surrounding the island and which appear at a glance to be elephants in the water. There are a number of ancient sites which have been preserved here as well as still occupied Nubian villages, the Aswan Museum and a large hotel (this is a big island) but due to time pressures we would simply sail around them and onward to Kitchener Island. This is the second major island and is named for Lord Kitchener who was given it as a reward for his services in the Sudan Campaign 1896-1898. His fame at the time derived from his leading role in a number of Imperial campaigns on behalf of the British Empire although he is best remembered now as the guy with a moustache who points out of the 'Your country needs YOU' poster. He worked with the Ministry of Irrigation and he quickly transformed the island into a paradise of exotic trees and plants interlaced with viewing walkways for the public. The entire island became, and still is, a Botanical Garden. The Egyptian government has taken ownership now and they have opened a research station on the southern end dedicated to experimenting with new cash crops and food sources but most of it is still open to the public as botanical gardens and it is hugely popular with the locals who can use it as a getaway from the city, perhaps for a weekend picnic or just a romantic stroll. We would just use it as a beautiful view to look at as we sailed past and on to the next location which was claimed to be the paddle steamer used in Death on the Nile but which I discovered after a little research wasn't. After a gentle couple of hours sailing about the river taking pictures of buildings for reasons that we now cannot recall we returned to the bank and found ourselves with a free afternoon to explore the city itself. For us there was only one destination that we wished to see and that is the Old Cataract Hotel. For those of you who are not fans of Death on the Nile this is the hotel that Poirot and the rest of the cast assemble at before departing on their river cruise to Wadi Halfa in Sudan. It is also the hotel where in real life Agatha Christie stayed while she was writing the book. It is an historic British colonial era hotel that is still a 5-star luxury resort. Originally built in 1899 by Thomas Cook (yes, the Thomas Cook of travel company fame) its purpose was to house European travellers who were very often on an Empire Tour. It has provided its services to the great and the good including Winston Churchill, Margaret Thatcher, Jimmy Carter, Princess Diana and Howard Carter who discovered the tomb of Tutankhamen. Three of the suites had been renamed the Agatha Christie Suite, The Winston Churchill Suite and the Howard Carter Suite in recognition of these famous guests. It was also a favoured destination of President Francois Mitterand of France who often opted to stay in the Winston Churchill Suite, which contains Churchill's original writing desk, and from where he loved to watch the sunset over the Nile valley. There is a swimming pool and terrace overlooking the river where you can bathe in the bathtub warm waters and take afternoon tea just as long as you are a guest. That was going to be a problem, you can only visit the hotel as a paying guest, you cannot turn up to have a tour, absolutely no non-residents allowed. We spoke to our tour guide about this and asked if there was any way round it and she looked a little bit uncomfortable at first but admitted under a little pressure that there was one option available, we could try bribing the security guards on the gate! Now we both like to think of ourselves as upstanding citizens and this was well outside of our comfort zone, we may well steal pens and post-it notes from work but that just compensates for the fact that work is shit, this was an entirely different league. Horrific visions of the next three months spent in an Egyptian jail while our loved ones shared our story on the evening news, probably with the least flattering photos they could find of us flashed up on the screen, flitted through our minds. Our Rep helpfully suggested that we could maintain a little distance from the actual act of bribery if we wandered into the streets, flagged down a taxi and explained to the driver where we wanted to go. She was sure that the driver would charge us an exaggerated taxi fare that would cover the necessary payments along with a handsome cut for himself and this would preserve the all important plausible deniability on our part if anything went wrong. What the hell we thought, you only live once and we really wanted to see it. The first driver was definitely not keen but with the second driver we quickly came to an understanding. Clearly sensing the opportunity to earn a months wages in one afternoon he gave us his price of £50. It didn't feel like a moment for bartering so we accepted this first offer and jumped in. Well, we would have jumped in except there were no handles on the rear doors. The door had to be lifted out of its resting place to allow us to enter and when slammed shut the window dropped inside the door. There was no handle to wind it back up but that didn't matter as the inside of the door was missing so you could just reach in and push the glass back up into place. We looked at each other and silently agreed that it was definitely worth it, assuming we survived. The hotel itself was only a short drive away and so within just a few minutes we were swinging into the drive and up to the security check point of the hotel. Our driver stopped the car and got out walking over to greet the guy on the gate as though old friends, there followed a brief but intense looking conversation at the end of which a nimble handshake transferred the bribe from the driver to the officer and we were in. Just like that. No fuss or bother at all.

The hotel was spectacular and as we approached up the drive it was easily recognisable from the film. This was from the scene where Lynett and Simon Doyle seek to outsmart the unbalanced Jacqueline De Bellefort by pretending to take a Kalesh (horse drawn carriage) to the railway station when in fact they would double back to the hotel to take the river cruise instead. I was excited and nervous in equal measure as our driver dropped us at the front door and told us that he would remain there until we were ready to be returned to our boat, the return fare already paid. He also informed us that now we were in we would be unchallenged as everyone working here would assume that we were guests and it was indeed so. We wandered around finding the ball room where Angela Lansbury and David Niven had performed their unique version of the Tango. We found the Agatha Christie and Howard Carter Suites with little trouble and then we headed out on to the terrace which overlooked the Nile. We headed to where Poirot had met with Simon Doyle on the banks of the river which was also Mitterand's favourite spot to sit and then we walked across and down the steps that would have led to the Karnak steamship on board of which the murder mystery would unfold. I was in heaven. A weird film nerd heaven granted but heaven none the less, but I began to feel that we shouldn't push our luck and having seen everything I had set out to see we headed back to our waiting driver.

We were pleased that our driver was actually waiting for us when we emerged and hadn't done a bunk with our pre-paid fare although we discovered that this was because he wanted to take us to his brother's souvenir shop on the way back and 'no' was not an acceptable answer. You may find if you ever travel to Egypt that most taxi rides involve a diversion to a relatives shop where you'll be shown assorted piles of tourist shit and genuine imitation antiquities. Happy with what we had seen that day we retired to the upper deck of the ship for a few drinks and to watch the lights of the city twinkling in the darkness, sitting there in the warm breeze of a desert evening, sipping gin & tonic and listening to the Call to Prayer resonating from the surrounding Mosques I could not have been happier. We would remain birthed in Aswan overnight as this was to be the base for some further excursions in the coming days. In the morning for example there was a big one. We were flying down to Abu Simbel!

We arrived at Aswan airport in the early hours of the morning and were swiftly herded in the direction of our plane. A plane I might add that would not have looked out of place in an episode of Aircrash Investigation on National Geographic. There was no safety briefing from the cabin crew, not that I noticed as I was to busy staring at the large crack running across the over-wing emergency exit hatch. The only thing missing was a piece of wood nailed across it at a jaunty angle. It seemed it would take the combined efforts of Harry Potter and Paul Daniels to get this crate safely off the ground and there was a palpable sense of relief throughout when we were finally airborne and the Cabin crew sprang to life and began distributing our breakfast. My other half decided this was the ideal time to have his morning bowel movement and disappeared to the back of the plane. Re-emerging a short while later he realised that the route back to his seat was soon to be cut off by the ever advancing cabin crew and their breakfast trolley. Not wishing to stand for the next twenty minutes he rushed back down the aircraft and managed to just jump into his seat squeezing past one of the crew as he did. Unfortunately he misjudged this manoeuvre and with his booted size 12 foot he managed to kick the stewardess hard on the ankle, right on that sensitive little bone that sticks out the side. To his considerable shock she let our a cry of pain that was so loud that everyone stopped what they were doing and turned to see what had happened. I had to screw my toes up in my shoes trying not to laugh as she clutched her ankle, tears in her eyes and began wailing,

"He kicked me, he kicked me, my ankle!"

The stewardess who was serving with her did not want to be left out of the action and joined in,

"What's happened, who kicked you?"

"He did, it was him!" the first stewardess wailed casting a filthy look in the direction of her new nemesis. Shaun responded by turning a stunning shade of bright red and began stuttering out repeated apologies while stressing that is was definitely an accident and he was really very sorry indeed. The entertainment eventually fizzled out as everyone regained their composure and I dropped my tray table ready for the food only to find it swung straight past the horizontal and down onto my legs. My only option was to lift my knees up in order to hold the table flat. Not that it was worth it as the breakfast consisted of weak ass orange juice in a little plastic cup which looked suspiciously like a urine sample and a ham sandwich. Calling it ham was overly generous considering the pale sweaty offering that I found in front of me and the words Mechanically Recovered Meat floated into my mind. All of this took place as we flew onward with pretty much the entire flight out over the desert alternating between sand and rock which created convection currents causing the plane to suddenly climb or drop several hundred feet without any discernible pattern or warning. I have never, and I mean never, been so grateful for a flight to end in my life.

Abu Simbel if you don't know is one of the most remarkable monuments in the world. Choose any word you like to describe it. Breathtaking, glorious, amazing, fabulous (That's like being amazing only with a sprinkle of glitter). There are two parts to the complex, the Great Temple and the Small Temple. The Great Temple is by far the most famous one and is carved into a cliff face with the façade standing 98 feet high and 115 feet long. There are four colossi, two on either side of the entrance, which are carved in the image of Ramesses II on his throne. Reciting facts and figures here does it no real justice unfortunately, the scale is simply so large its difficult to comprehend just how imposing it is. As you stand gazing at it your sense of perspective becomes distorted and it seems smaller and closer to you than it actually is and only when you walk towards it do you begin to comprehend, only then as you crane your neck back to take it all in do you really appreciate what an achievement it is.

There is some disagreement over when this temple was constructed as well as over the origin of its name. It was constructed sometime between 1264BC and 1224BC depending on which scholar you happen to be reading. One group believe it may have been built at the earlier date to celebrate a great victory over the Hittites at the Battle of Kadesh as indicated by the art work inside. The other group believe that its location means that it must have been built after the Nubian campaigns which Ramasses II undertook with his sons and it exists as a symbol of Egypt's power. As for the name it is claimed that the temple was first discovered by a Swiss explorer called Burckhardt who was led to the site by a young boy called Abu Simbel in 1813AD and he named the site after him. Burckhardt had studied at Cambridge University and as a bona-fide explorer led numerous expeditions throughout Africa and the Middle East. Alternatively it could have been Giovanni Belzoni who arrived in 1817AD and who excavated the entrance area that named it, a man whom some consider an Egyptologist and whom others consider a grave robber. He set out as a young man to join a monastic order but ended up as a circus strong-man who built model hydraulic engines. Naturally he then headed off to explore Egypt! All that is known for certain is if there was a specific name for the complex when it was built then it has now been lost in the mists of time. Amazingly, or at least I think its amazing, the temple is so constructed that twice a year on the 21st of February and the 21st of October the sun shines directly into the inner sanctuary illuminating the statues of Ramesses and the god Amun. There is a third statue in there as well of the god Ptah of the Egyptian underworld but this one is positioned so that it is kept in endless darkness. Pretty neat. Looking at this massive construction its hard to believe that it has only been in this location since the late 1960's. The Government at that time planned to build the Aswan High Dam which would have resulted in both of these temples being submerged under the newly created Lake Nasser. Under the threat of losing such a monument a multi-million dollar operation was spearheaded by UNESCO in which both temples were dismantled and moved over 200 feet upwards onto the plateau of the cliffs they once sat below. UNESCO is a United Nations Organisation that seeks to promote peace in the world on the basis of humanity's moral and intellectual solidarity, or so it says on their web page. They assembled an international team of archaeologists and secured the funding to undertake this behemoth of a task. Both temples were rebuilt some 700 feet to the north-west of their original location in a man-made mountain to maintain the impression of the temples being cut into the cliff face all the while taking great care to ensure that their orientation to the sun remained exact. Before they could start their work it was necessary to build what was called a coffer dam which protected the temples from the rapidly rising waters. The next step was to actually saw the temples into individual blocks with every effort made to make the cuts in those areas where they would be least visible. A framework constructed from concrete was used to hold the internal walls and ceiling in place and the outside blocks were reassembled using a mortar made of cement and desert sand which was finished so well that today they are invisible to an amateur eye. The mountain in which they now stand is artificially constructed with rubble being piled on top of two vast domes of reinforced concrete which when you see the size of them is simple astonishing.

I should think by any ones estimation the sheer scale of this project matches the original construction of the temples themselves. Abu Simbel became the second most visited site in Egypt after the Pyramids of Giza and this place is in the middle of nowhere and requires its own airport to support the tourists who visit here every year. On your arrival all you see is the back of the artificial mountain and two paths lead away around either side. As you follow these paths you see in front of you the enormous expanse of lake Nasser and as you turn the final corner the temple façade comes into view. Shaun said afterwards that it is the only time in his life when something he saw was so spectacular that it actually took his breath away. I'm not eulogising here, we were left speechless by the appearance of this place. The panoramic view in front of us was magnificent and its setting on the banks of Lake Nasser suits it perfectly even though most of the pictures you'll see of it carefully edit out the lakeside location. There is scene in Death on the Nile which contrives to make it appear as though it is in the middle of the desert and you wouldn't for a moment suspect that it's bang on top of one of the largest man-made lakes in the world.

Having run out of time we began the walk back to the coach, occasionally pausing for a last lingering look until we rounded the corner and it fell out of sight. Arriving back at the coach on time and well ahead of everyone else for some reason we found ourselves with a little unexpected free time. Shaun decided to make use of this time by plunging into a nearby market from where he could barter for a scale model of the temple carved in onyx, a model that still has a prominent place in our living room today. In contrast I decided to use the time to evacuate my bowels before boarding the coach for the long return journey. Now as anyone who knows me will testify I will shit anywhere. From Windsor Castle and the Romanian Parliament to 'drop toilets' in the Australian outback and communal toilets in central China, I'm not bothered. Thanks to one particularly pleasing mid-morning bowel movement in New York I can still claim to have left my breakfast at Tiffanys. With such extensive knowledge of all things lavatorial I can state without fear of contradiction that the toilets here in Abu Simbel were amongst the worst in the world. Consisting of a small Porta-Cabin set off to one side they were filthy with dubious looking stains liberally smeared across the walls. Fetid water, or at least mainly water slopped around the floor and was just deep enough to splash as you walked and begin soaking into the fabric of your hiking boots. Just to complete the effect a stench like a truckers gusset assaulted your nasal passageways and made you literally gasp for breath, slipping the neck of your t-shirt up over your nose provided only minimal relief. An enterprising lady was sat inside on a small stool where she had stockpiled all the available toilet paper. Her price was one Egyptian pound which purchased precisely one sheet of toilet paper. The Egyptian pound is still a paper note and the surface area of it is somewhat larger than the single sheet of toilet paper. I'd have been better off using the currency to wipe my arse and by the look of most of the notes other people had done exactly that. Once we had both completed our business it was time to make the journey back to the boat for a little relaxation before the rigours of the next day.

It was on that next day that we headed off to Philae temple for no less than two visits. Philae has also been saved from the rising waters of the Nile. It was originally located near the river's first cataract (the cataracts are shallow lengths of the river where the water is broken by small boulders sticking out of the river bed and creating a white water effect) but the construction of the old Aswan Dam in 1902 led to the area being flooded on a regular basis. UNESCO were again involved in the dismantling and relocation of the entire temple complex to a nearby island called Agilkia thus protecting it from any further damage. The Old Dam was constructed by the British who had invaded and occupied Egypt in 1882 but the idea of creating a dam on the Nile dates back to the 11th century. The enormous technical difficulties meant that the British project, built between 1898 and 1902, was the first successful venture. It was also the largest masonry dam constructed in the world at that time and nothing even approaching the scale of it had ever been attempted before. Even so it proved inadequate and its height was raised twice over the next thirty years until it was realised that a new dam, the Aswan High Dam, would have to be constructed a few miles upstream. In order to reach Philae on its island we had to cross by boat on which the health and safety was so poor that we were compelled to take our life jackets with us from the Commodore. There's nothing like living life on the edge. The temple here was built in honour of the Goddess and Queen known as Isis and the priestesses who led her worship became famed as skilled midwives and healers of ailments. It was believed that they were in control of great magic which they used for healing as well as being able to control the weather simply by combing their hair. Now I know that last bit sounds a bit bonkers but you would be amazed at how common that particular piece of superstition is. Sailors from the Romans to the Royal Navy, from the Caribbean to the Tasman sea have held the belief that cutting your hair whilst at sea in calm conditions may provoke foul weather to descend. In Scotland it was believed that even if your not on a ship but one of your relatives is then cutting your hair will have the same effect. It is my strong suspicion that with large numbers of sailors together on one ship the chances of someone not having had a haircut within a day or so of a storm beginning are remote. Isis was held to be responsible for the weather and was in control of the sky as well as being associated with life after death. She may well have been responsible for the ritual of mummification as she sought survival and power in the afterlife for her and her family, an afterlife where it is believed she would guard the Canopic jars which contained the removed organs of the mummified and an afterlife where she would act as a guide to the deceased on their journey.

The temple dominates this island, just as it dominates the surrounding river and its structure spreads over a quarter of the available area. After leaving our little boat and walking up into the temple one of the first things to be seen is not Egyptian but French, and that thing is a large piece of graffiti carved into the walls of the temple. It was placed there by the Commission des Sciences at des Arts in 1799 to mark what was supposed to be a high point in French military endeavours. The French campaign in Egypt had sealed Napoleon's reputation as a great military genius and statesmen. His arrival with an expeditionary force in Alexandria just one year before had quickly seen local opposition routed, particularly at the decisive battle of the pyramids. The routed Mamaluke forces had then been pursued by a division of French forces led by General Desaix, the very same soldiers who had taken the brunt of the Mamaluke attack at the pyramids and they were chased south and out of Egypt. It is during this pursuit that the aforementioned graffiti was added to the temple. As well as guiding his forces to supposed pre-eminence across Europe Napoleon's Egyptian campaign allowed his propaganda machine to go into overdrive. He could claim this victory dealt a blow to the British who's supply lines to India now had to be diverted down around the bottom of Africa. With this weakening of Britain's position surely the French forces in India, that great jewel of the east, would soon make it their own. Against this near hysterical rising of expectations Napoleon engineered a coup-de-tat in November 1799 and claimed the title of First Consul of the Republic making France and its dominions his to lead. The only problem with this reading of the situation is that it is not entirely true and that is thanks to the British Royal Navy and a certain Horatio Nelson of Battle of Trafalgar fame.

Whatever victories that the French army could achieve in Egypt were of little and certainly of no lasting consequence because they were cut-off, isolated, alone. At the start of august in 1798 a taskforce of fourteen British ships commanded by Nelson sited the French fleet of seventeen warships in Aboukir Bay just along the coast from Alexandria. The French were in a strong defensive position close into the shore and with additional protection from gun batteries on a nearby island. It was late in the day and the light was already beginning to fade and that coupled with their defensive position led Vice-Admiral Francois-Paul Brueys d'Aigalliers to believe that there was no chance that the British would be foolish enough to attack and so no preparations were made. Unfortunately for him Rear Admiral Sir Horatio Nelson was quick with his judgement and was always prepared for swift action. He wasted not a single moment in committing his entire naval force to the attack in spite of the enemies superior numbers and defensive position. The French were at anchor in a line so Nelson split his force into two with him leading the ships seaward and the remaining ships slipping through a gap between the first French ship and the shore. D'Aigalliers ships found themselves trapped in a cross-fire at close quarters with no way out. By the end of the battle only two of the big French battle ships managed to slip away accompanied by two smaller frigates, the only four to escape that night. Orient, the flagship of the fleet had exploded and gone to the bottom along with six other vessels and the remaining six were captured and taken back as the spoils of war. D'Aigalliers faced no consequences for his terrible lapse of judgement as he didn't survive the night whereas Nelson found his reputation made. This one battle completely reversed the strategic position in the Mediterranean with the balance of power tilted decisively in favour of the British. By 1801 the French army was being evacuated from Egypt, British supply lines to India were secure as was their military position there and the French naval forces were a shadow of their former self and didn't challenge Britain's supremacy for the rest of the war. The news was received with such rapture back home that he was given a peerage and became Baron Nelson of the Nile along with having a generous pension bestowed upon him by a grateful parliament.

That background, knowing that bit of history made that French graffiti rather poignant for me. Here is a boast carved in stone I thought, a memorial which they left to demonstrate their superiority and yet all the pieces were already in place for their decline and defeat at the hands of the British not only in Egypt but on the high seas and in Europe as well. Talk about Hubris.

Our second visit was in the late evening after it had dropped dark and we were all invited to take our seats in the centre of the island for a light and sound show. For the next hour the temple was brought to life with a mixture of illumination, music and booming voices on an audio track which gave a colourful if brief overview of the trials and tribulations of the local gods. Should you ever find yourself travelling here and you would like to learn more of the stories that surround these ancient gods then this show is a splendid way to do it, although I have to say there was no mention throughout the show of Human sacrifice and it had been my understanding that Philae temple was at the epicentre of this in ancient times although it turns out this is a controversial and much discussed question with many people particularly in Egypt vigorously denying the possibility. The ancient Egyptians were certainly not squeamish when it came to blood and gore. The heads of enemy warriors who were captured and sentenced to death would be beaten until the skull was crushed and the head burst open or alternately they may have had a large spike driven up their bum hole. Some tombs have been found to contain remains where the throat shows signs of being cut before the head was decapitated and some depictions show victims holding a bowl to catch their own blood as it spilled out of their jugular. At the necropolis of Abydos in the burial complex of King Aha an excavation found thirty-six graves all of which contained the bodies of young men in their early 20's. The fact that so many bodies are all found buried together and at such a uniform age would suggest that they were killed for the purpose rather than dying of natural causes, strangulation being most likely as they showed no signs of having their throats slit and the skeletons were all found in the same position which rules out being buried alive. If they had been buried alive it seems most unlikely they would have all lain quietly waiting for death, one would imagine some screaming and banging on the coffin lid with a growing sense of urgency would have been likely. Some deaths could be a little more niche, tailored to the recipient as it were, such as Hypatia of Alexandria who was stripped, beaten to death with stone tiles, dismembered and then set on fire. You could argue that these examples are not sacrifices to the Gods, rather they come under the headings of punishments, acts of war or as in the case of the servants it was for the benefit of their master who they would continue to serve in the afterlife. I merely make the point that although the idea of human sacrifice may be controversial the Egyptians were not uncomfortable about death and over the span of their history it seems unlikely that no human sacrifices would have been made to the gods. Academic sources supporting the existence of these practices are numerous even if the physical evidence is somewhat more difficult to come by. The historian Procopius who lived in the 6th century had written of Philae and the barbarous temple cults that existed there would sacrifice humans to restore cosmic balance until the emperor Justinian had interceded and brought an end to it. The German Egyptologist Hermann Junker concluded in the early 20th century that from the representations of that period which showed hippopotamus, bulls and human figures being sacrificed that human sacrifice was practiced and may have been imported from the Nubians. Just after the Second World War the historian J.G. Griffiths presented a review of the classical evidence and concluded that human sacrifice definitely occurred at certain times and within certain cults but was not widespread in the way it was with the Aztecs for example. As for why they needed to restore cosmic balance it all comes down to our old friend Set, the testicle free god who for some reason best known to himself killed King Osiris, husband of Isis, thus introducing death to our world and creating an imbalance that only an offering to the gods can negate. Of all of this you will hear nothing during your light and sound show but I think it's definitely worth learning about.

Our last excursion from Aswan where we had now been for three days was to the Aswan High Dam itself. I have mentioned it a few times but now I was actually going to get to see it. The scale of this project is astounding standing 364 feet high (more than one and half times the wingspan of a Boeing 747), it is 12,562 feet across at its top (the Empire State Building in New York is 1250 feet tall) and has a volume of nearly 58 million cubic yards (The Hoover Dam has less than 4.5 million). This thing is big! It also has a road running across it which is much used by various lorries and vans, I know this because whilst not paying attention I stepped in front of one of them. The finger marks in my shoulder where I was grabbed and pulled to safety were still visible a month later. When you stand on top of it and look South in the direction of Sudan you realise that as big as the Dam is it is dwarfed by Lake Nasser, the reservoir that it has created. The Lake stretches back nearly 200 miles to the Egyptian/Sudanese border and then on into Sudan for another 100 miles. This is the reservoir that required the moving of Abu Simbel as well as requiring that ninety thousand people be resettled away from their homes across two countries. The original British Dam was unable to hold back the annual Nile flood so a series of sluice gates allowed it to wash straight through every year and so in the 1950's the leader of Egypt, Gamal Abdel Nasser envisioned the construction of a new mightier Dam that would tame the flood once and for all and allow man to control the river for the first time and simultaneously providing an enormous source of cheap, clean electricity from which the whole of the country could benefit. The benefits are immediately obvious and when weighted against the construction costs it was an obvious choice to pursue the development but what they didn't take into account were the long term costs and environmental impact of its construction. It was the 1950's though and a disregard for the environment would not have been peculiar to the Egyptians. The flood waters that came every year also brought rich fertile soil from upstream which it deposited along the banks of the river downstream. Without this annual renewal of the soil the fertility levels have dropped substantially and farmers now face massive additional costs to fertilize their own land. The stability of the water table and the resulting process of irrigation has led to some areas becoming waterlogged and other areas getting saturated with salt rendering them useless for agriculture. The level of nutrients flowing from the river into the Mediterranean was also reduced dramatically and this had a direct impact on the fishing industry, for example the sardine catch off the Egyptian coast dropped from 18,000 tons in 1962 to less than 500 tons in 1968 since when it has rebounded but has never climbed back above 10,000 tons. The last thing that our guide told us about, and I am sure there is plenty more, is that the reduction in sediment has made the Nile a much clearer river which allows sunlight to penetrate much more deeply, coupled with all the fertilizers that are now being used (which run off into the river) there has been an explosion in the level of algae which has rendered the water even less drinkable and more expensive to treat than before the High Dam was built. This is the exact opposite outcome of what all the experts had expected and these are only a few of the consequences. One does wonder if all the reassurances about fracking in the U.K. are so much bunkum as well!

Anyway back to Nasser and his grand plan. He may not have realised it at the time but another unexpected consequence of his project was the 'Suez Crisis' which was one of the few times that the Cold War actually started to hot up a bit. Originally he had intended to pay for the project with the financial backing of the United States and Great Britain but in July 1956 the crisis began to unfold. The western powers learned of a secret arms deal negotiated by Nasser with the U.S.S.R. and given the Cold War tensions which prevailed the response was swift and the agreement to finance the Dam was cancelled. The dominos began to fall as Nasser responded by Nationalising the British and French owned Suez Canal with the intention of using the revenue from all that shipping to pay for his project instead, while at the same time delivering a significant strategic set-back to the once mighty Europeans. Britain and France were incensed by this and ignoring the pleas for peace from their allies they decided to go to war. They found an ally in Israel who thought that a Nasser led Egypt backed by the Soviets was a serious threat to their security and so they agreed to invade Egypt as a pretext to allow Britain and France to send in their forces as 'peace-keepers' to restore order. On October 29th 1956 Israel attacked and a joint ultimatum was issued by the British and French demanding an immediate ceasefire, a ceasefire that the Israelis duly ignored. The die was cast and on November 5th the Anglo-French paratrooper forces landed and took control. Their success in swiftly occupying the canal zone was soon to turn to humiliation at the hands of their ally the United States. It became obvious that the entire thing had been planned beforehand and President Eisenhower wanted to distance himself from what he saw as an act of colonialism and so he joined forces (diplomatically rather than militarily) with the Russians and the United Nations forcing Britain and France into a withdrawal and handing the Suez Canal over to Egyptian control. Nasser was greatly strengthened and the revenue gained from the Canal along with some Soviet backed loans enabled him to complete his great project and the reservoir was named after him in honour of his achievement. Whilst he was enjoying the adulation of the Egyptian people back in Britain the crisis precipitated the downfall of Prime Minister Anthony Eden. For three decades he had enjoyed a reputation as a safe pair of hands on foreign policy, holding the position of Foreign Secretary from 1935-1938, then during the Second World War from 1940-1945 and again from 1951-1955 after which he ascended to Number 10. Ironic then that it should be foreign policy that would destroy his Premiership and leave his reputation in shreds less than two years later. He resigned on the 9th January 1957 on the grounds of poor health, which was true, but the debacle he had presided over had made his position untenable anyway.

Speaking of military matters the Egyptian military were very much in evidence around the site today and for good reason. If any hostile power or terrorist organisation wanted to launch an attack there is not a single place where the country is more vulnerable. David was in his element now as he outlined the nightmare scenario of the High Dam being breeched unleashing the waters of Lake Nasser. The scale of the disaster would be beyond anything that has ever gone before. Worse than the worst natural disaster, worse than Chernobyl or Fukushima, worse than tsunamis or ebola. The death toll within one day of its destruction would rival the entirety of World War 2. The highest point of Cairo would be underwater with everything and everyone on the way utterly destroyed by the force of the water. All in all this seemed a good justification for the large military presence we witnessed who were clearly a very sensible precaution. As we stood there on a sunny afternoon, taking in the structure and the calm blue waters of the lake beyond it gave us a moments pause. With that thought bouncing around our heads we headed back to the coach in order to return to our ship. Tonight we would sail, reversing direction and heading back to Luxor.

We had only one more stop before our cruise would be over and that was at the temple at Dendra. To get there we had to again pass through the locks at Esna and with little else to do we decided to stand on deck and watch our progress through the lock. We stood quietly watching our approach until a shrill and repeated blast of a whistle broke the silence.

"I wonder what that's…" Shaun began but before he could finish the Commodore hit the jetty with a jolt that had us scrabbling for a handrail as the entire boat rolled to an angle of about forty-five degrees. Ok, maybe ten degrees but it feels worse when your on it believe me. Most of the water in the swimming pool took the opportunity to escape in one very large wave which swept over the deck and away into the river drenching some unfortunate passengers who had been foolish enough to stand about three metres to the left of where we were. The Commodore quickly righted itself and was repositioned to head through the gates. Wanting to calm himself down my other half decided to have a cigarette and as we nosed our way into the lock he took out a packet and was immediately spotted by members of the Tourist Police who were on the ground three decks below us. They began gesturing to him making it quite clear that they wished to 'bum a smoke'. He only had two left in the packet so he figured what the hell and threw it down to them. His generosity was unappreciated and the officers made it quite clear through hand gestures alone that as a wealthy western tourist the least he could do is throw them down a full packet which when you think about it is a lot to convey through hand gestures. They were clearly well practiced. Feeling somewhat affronted and definitely unappreciated he dismissed there demands which a hand gesture of his own with which he had also had much practice. This would have probably been fine if it weren't for the fact that at that very moment the waters of the lock began to drain and we started to sink closer and closer to their level necessitating a tactical withdrawal back inside the bar until we were safely on our way again.

We arrived at the Temple of Hathor in Dendera the next day and found the place had two outstanding points in its favour. The first was the fact that you could climb up onto the roof from where a stunning panorama of the surrounding countryside was visible. Unfortunately there are no barriers or walls around the edge of the roof, just a sheer drop to the floor below, and in 2004 a lady fell off the highest section of the temple and was killed. That section was closed to the public after the accident but other areas of the roof are still open and accessible by the original and somewhat time worn spiral staircase. Secondly this is the temple that was used as Karnak Temple in the most recent production of Death on the Nile starring David Suchet. They wisely chose not to emulate the 1978 film too closely choosing different filming locations and most certainly dialling down the overall campness (in spite of Frances De La Tour's performance as Madame Otterbourne). David spoke warmly of the place and felt it was underappreciated when it is regarded as one of the best preserved temples in the whole of Egypt. It was an important site for the cult of Hathor and includes brick vaulted catacombs which are the resting place for many birds and dogs which occupied an important place in the local mythology. They have also found numerous cows buried around the necropolis, all treated with great care and respect because the form of the cow was also very important to their beliefs. When we visited the temple the inside was blackened with soot from several centuries of Bedouins camping and building fires for warmth and to heat their cooking pots. Since we visited a large scale cleaning program has been undertaken to remove the soot without damaging the delicate colours underneath. I have only seen photos of the work but if they do it any justice the overall effect in their must be breathtaking. There also used to be a large sculpted zodiac suspended from the ceiling of the Greco-Roman temple but in the eighteenth century some enterprising explorers hacked it off after which it found its way to Le Louvre in Paris. They have replaced it with a replica but the knowledge that it's a fake does rather reduce its impact and raises questions about the ethical code of the explorers and the Egyptian ruler of the time, Mohamed Ali Pasha, who gave permission for its transportation. It is not the Zodiac in the modern astrological sense but rather an actual depiction of the night sky at the time. There was some genuine excitement from David as he informed us that an Astrophysicist who studied it discovered that the five planets represented were in a formation which only occurs once every thousand years and was therefore able to date it to between 15th June and 15th August 50 B.C. which I think is pretty remarkable. It even portrays a solar eclipse which it interprets as the goddess Isis holding a baboon (the god Thoth) by its tail which is her attempt to stop the moon hiding the sun. It is an accurate map of the sky but the Egyptians did believe that those constellations could have a negative influence on their health and their destiny in much the same way modern astrology claims to be able to foretell your future by the positions of the planet. The fact that it is all a pile of utter hokum should not for one minute reduce your enjoyment of it or your appreciation of the skill involved in its creation.

Although that was to be the end of our cruise we still had one more day of excursions to enjoy before leaving the Commodore for good. I put on some trousers and a shirt that I had not worn since the start of the holiday (I always pack light and am not above getting a second or even third days use out of clothes) and discovered that they were not as commodious as they had been at the start of the week. It would seem that my waistline had expanded by a noticeable amount in the week we had been here. In hindsight this made sense as we were getting virtually no exercise, they fed us three times a day with extra snacks and tea & tiffin every afternoon and we drank a day's worth of calories in alcohol every night. I considered changing and then decided I couldn't be bothered and un-tucked my shirt, pushed my waistband below my distended stomach and headed out.

Today we would be visiting the Valleys! More specifically the Valley of the Kings and the Valley of the Queens as well as the Temple of Hatshepsut which are all clustered together in an area on the west bank of the Nile. This entire area was to be a necropolis or 'city of the dead' where the Kings, Queens and significant other persons would be buried. This area was not chosen at random but because it stands underneath a mountain called 'Dehent' (the peak) or as it's known in Arabic 'el-Qurn' (the horn). This mountain is a natural pyramid and is likely an echo of the pyramids that were built under the Old Kingdom, the belief being that the pyramid acts as a 'stargate' allowing the souls of the dead to ascend to their place in heaven (somewhere near Ursa Minor apparently!) This area was used as a necropolis from the 16th to the 11th centuries BC, a period of some 500 years of construction and burial by the people of the New Kingdom and it now provides some of the most famous archaeological sites anywhere in the world. Our first visit was the Valley of the Kings which contains a total of 63 tombs varying in size from a simple pit to a gargantuan complex of 120 chambers. Discoveries of new chambers and tomb entrances still happen with the most recent being in 2008 although the unrest in Egypt has seriously impeded the work over the last few years. We were to take the coach up to the entrance where a visitor centre had been constructed. This was a squat, plain white building with little to commend it. There were some toilets, a small shop to purchase drinks, snacks and souvenirs and a restaurant which was closed. There was also no air conditioning and the design appeared to concentrate the suns rays into the buildings interior where the temperature had risen far above the outside. There were no fans, no breeze, no respite. David told us that we had some free time as we were waiting for transport to arrive so we purchased some drinks and headed outside where we could wait in the cool shade at the rear of the building. It was while we were here that we noticed something surprising. Either side of the road that led up into the valley were a series of small pits around three feet deep. If they were deliberately dug or naturally occurring I'm unsure but I do know that what was in them was not natural by any means. Rubbish! Lots and lots of rubbish and I mean real shitty rubbish. Alongside empty bottles and crisp wrappers were discarded and stained clothing, used nappies, tissues, bandages and plasters. This was a dumping ground. This historic site was a dumping ground for any bit of detritus that people wished to discard. My heart sank when I saw this and there was a real sense of disappointment that not only had this been allowed to happen but also that no effort had been made to clean any of it up. It was perfectly clear that this stuff had been sitting and festering here for some time right next to where all the tourists would be trooping through every day. Why did no one care? I can hardly imagine being required to pass through this on your way to Chatsworth House back in Derbyshire. As we contemplated this our transport arrived which consisted of a small tractor that had been made up to look like a steam engine pulling several trailers which I believed were supposed to look like the carriages. The whole thing appeared as though it had been involved in a fatal accident in the past but had been pressed back into service anyway. We boarded along with the rest of our group and spent the next five minutes choking on the black cloud of diesel fumes pouring out of the knackered old tractor as it attempted to drag the weight of its five carriages filled with tourists up the incline to our final destination. As was usually the case the arrival made everything else we had experienced worthwhile. The valley is stunning, bathed in golden sunshine, topped with clear electric blue sky, the peak of el-Qurn visible above us and marked out in every direction the entrances to the tombs of the dead Kings. We would have the opportunity to visit three of the tombs today but the one we were really excited about was Tutankhamen. Who hasn't heard of the curse of Tutankhamen and who wouldn't want to see it for themselves. Tutankhamen, the boy king, is probably the most well known of all the pharaohs of ancient Egypt but was in fact only a minor figure in that history. His fame rests far more on the discovery, or rediscovery, of his tomb in 1922 and the stories and legends that surround it. The tomb was discovered by Howard Carter (it was his suite I sought out at the Old Cataract Hotel in Aswan). Howard Carter's interest in the field of Egyptology was first ignited by his father Samuel Carter in a roundabout sort of way. His father was a successful artist and one day he was asked to paint the portrait of a well know Egyptologist called Lord Amherst. When visiting Amherst's mansion he took his young son along who witnessed a large collection of Egyptian antiquities there. The young Howard Carter's interest was aroused and he never looked back. He secured his first placement on a dig in Egypt in 1891 at the age of only 17, he then joined the Egyptian Antiquities Service and spent six years in their employment until he got into a dispute with some French tourists who complained to his employers. Carter was ordered to apologise but refused resulting first in his demotion and then ultimately in his resignation. He had a tough few years after this having to work as an artist to support himself but it did prove fortuitous however as it led to him being introduced to Lord Carnarvon, an eager amateur Egyptologist who was keen to provide Carter with all the funds he would need to continue his work independently. It was this relationship that would lead to the discovery of Tutankhamen's Tomb. Lord Carnarvon was a wealthy man with deep pockets who could well afford to support the project and you can tell this just from looking at his home. His family's estate is Highclere Castle in Berkshire which most people would more readily recognise as Downton Abbey from the program of the same name. Any one who could afford to live there would clearly have no trouble financing a little expedition to Egypt. The donation was not entirely philanthropic anyway as many of the treasures that were pulled from the graves were shipped back to Highclere for Carnarvon's personal collection. If you visit the house now you will still find an Egyptian exhibit but I'm pleased to say that it consists only of replicas as all the real treasure has been returned. I wasn't so pleased on the day we visited when I spent an extra £20 on the tickets to enter the exhibit and realised it was only copies of things I had already seen for real (Still worth going though).

Carter undertook to supervise the excavations that were sponsored and was given overall direction by Carnarvon and he had some success securing a number of antiquities for the personal collection by 1914. This was not what Carter was after though, his dream was to discover the tomb of Tutankhamen which he believed had not yet been found. He was very much in a minority in this belief as back in 1905 an American Egyptologist by the name of Theodore Davis had unearthed a tomb (the 58th tomb found) which consisted of a single chamber and a cache of gold foils with Tutankhamen's name on them. The small size of the chamber was consistent with the age of the boy king when he dies. The tombs construction commences when a king takes over the throne and the longer they serve the bigger the tombs will become. With Tutankhamen dying at only 19 it was to be expected that the tomb would be small and unimpressive. Carter didn't believe it for a minute and pressed ahead with his search, certain in the belief that the real chamber was still to be found and would contain many 'wonderful things', his words. For six seasons they searched the valley back and forth, exploring every potentially forgotten place but with no luck. Eventually even Lord Carnavon gave up and went back to England but Carter did persuade him to provide the funds for one last search and it's a good job he did. In that sixth year of searching he finally made the discovery that he was so desperate for. David told us that there was a large sandstorm overnight and on the morning of November 1st 1922 Carter awoke to discover that the storm had swept away the sand over a platform in the corner of his tent. This platform was found to be the first step leading down to the tomb and he realised he had been camping on top of the entrance the whole time. That version may be bullshit and he in fact discovered the tomb without any meteorological intervention but personally I find David's version a lot more satisfying. A telegram was dispatched back to his patron which read;

'At last have made wonderful discovery in valley; a magnificent tomb with seals intact, re-covered same for your arrival; congratulation.'

He did indeed re-cover the tomb and had to then wait for over two weeks until Carnarvon could travel back out to him and they could enter the tomb together. It was on the 26th of November that he finally got to make a hole in the sealed doorway and saw inside the sealed tomb for the first time. It was magnificent, it had been so completely lost that no grave robbers had got to it and the collection inside was still in tact. It was not large as was expected and it was hastily completed but it was still full to bursting with treasure upon treasure. Many of the replicas in the display at Highclere are of the finds in here, with many of the originals residing at the Egyptian Museum in Cairo. Possibly the most famous find of all is the Death Mask of the young king made from precious stones, glass and gold. It resides in a glass case in a dedicated room at the museum in Cairo and when we visited a series of spotlights illuminated it in the centre of its large glass case to stunning effect. In 2014 I am very sorry to say it was discovered that the Death Mask had been damaged as its beard had become detached and some idiot attempted to reattach it with a strong adhesive.

The repair was cavalier, the damage clearly visible with a gap between the face and the beard and some of the adhesive spoiling the delicate colours of the beard itself. The last I heard eight employees of the museum had given somewhat different accounts as to what had happened and they had all been charged with not following proper protocols and were awaiting trial. New experts were drafted in to fix the mask but I believe that the lighting effect which was so thrilling when we were there has had to be toned down so as to make the repair invisible to the casual observer. The tombs of all these great kings were filled with treasures of course including precious metals and gems but there was also a great deal more. Some ancient Egyptian burials would also include mummified beef ribs, sliced duck and goat meat in order to provide a meal for the deceased in the afterlife which is very considerate. There would also be furniture so as to make them comfortable along with games to keep them occupied and the casting of magic spells to keep them safe. From the pre-dynastic period of their history there were also gender differences in the contents of the tombs with males finding themselves facing the afterlife with a selection of handy weapons whereas the women would have to make do with a selection of cosmetics. It was during the time of the Old Kingdom that mummification of the bodies became normal practice with linen bandages and possibly moulded plaster used to wrap the bodies before they were placed into the sarcophagi to be interred. This also heralded the arrival of the Canopic containers in which the deceased's internal organs would be stored for the journey to the next world although I am still a little unclear as to how removing them from the body was going to improve things for their owner in the afterlife. Pretty hard to enjoy the sliced duck when your stomach is in a jar six feet away. These pots and the sarcophagus would often be the only items found that were specifically made for the burial with everything else being the everyday items owned by the individual that they wished to take with them and continue using. If they didn't have something they felt they would need in the afterlife, no problem, just etch a relief of the item you need into the walls of the tomb and the depiction will become manifest in the next life!

The discovery of the tomb was a media sensation at the time and the people involved quickly became household names but within a few short years the story was to take a sinister twist. Lord Carnarvon died on the 5th of April 1923 from an infected mosquito bite. The curse of the mummy's tomb was resurrected in the public consciousness. There was in fact no curse found inscribed in the tomb but this did not stop the story. On the 16th of May 1923 one George Jay Gould died from a fever after visiting the tomb; in July another visitor Prince Ali Kamel Fahmy Bey died after being shot by his wife; in September Carnarvon's half brother developed blood poisoning from a dental procedure and passed away; on the 15th January 1924 the radiologist who had x-rayed the mummy, Sir Archibald Douglas-Reid, died from a mysterious illness; November 1924 Sir Lee Stack, another visitor and Governor General of Sudan, was assassinated in Cairo; in 1928 A.C.Mace a member of the excavation team died from arsenic poisoning; 1929 and The Hon. Mervyn Herbert, Carnarvon's half brother, died from Malarial pneumonia and Carters personal secretary, Captain Richard Bethell, died from self administered poisoning in bed and his father threw himself off the seventh floor of his apartment block the next year. Finally Howard Carter himself passed away in 1939, over 15 years later, but his death too was attributed to the 'curse' by some observers. There was also a story that Carter gave a paperweight to his friend Sir Bruce Ingram which was a mummified hand with a bracelet which said;

'cursed be he who moves my body. To him shall come fire, water and pestilence'

Soon after receiving the gift his house burnt down and after he completed its rebuilding it flooded. Now I am not for a moment suggesting that the curse is real and in fact if you look at the number of people who were involved with or visited the site the number of people who suffered a misfortune or early death is no greater than any large randomly picked group of people. Even so it makes a bloody good story. Having been suitably spooked David ushered us back up the short flight of stairs and on to the next stop.

We were to discover that time has not been kind to any of these tombs. Although they were buried as were many of the temples they have suffered at the hands of treasure hunters (grave robbers to be more precise), floods and more recently have deteriorated significantly due to the mass tourism of which we were a part. Every tourist leaves around 3 grams of sweat behind in every tomb they visit and this moisture has caused enormous damage to the delicate pigments which were used to decorate the walls of the chambers. Speaking for myself in the stiflingly hot interior of this place 3 grams seems a decidedly conservative estimate. David explained to us that our very breath was also detrimental as with every exhale we raised the level of carbon dioxide inside the tomb causing yet more damage. In order to tackle these threats a rota system has been introduced closing the tombs in turn for restoration work alongside the installation of de-humidifiers and glass screens in the worst affected areas.

We headed on to the next tomb which was Merenptah and I paused only briefly to adjust my belt which was becoming deeply uncomfortable and rather put me in mind of that piece of string you get round a beef joint. This was but the work of a moment and we soon arrived at the next destination.

Merenptah was the 13th son of Ramses II and didn't become king until he was well into his sixties. His father had lasted so long on the throne that all twelve of his older siblings had died before having the opportunity to succeed him. This was the largest tomb that we were to see and is the second largest tomb in the whole valley. This long tomb has suffered a good deal of water damage from flooding to the lower parts of its walls but some of the upper parts are well preserved and still impressive. These tombs have been discovered and opened before as the Coptic and Greek graffiti scrawled about the place helpfully proves but much of it fortunately remains intact and unspoilt. We were shown a false burial chamber containing two pillars decorated with the Book of Gates and corridors also decorated with the Book of Gates as well as the Book of the Dead and the Book of Amduat. These are all funereal in nature. Amduat was reserved only for the Pharaohs and was a guide to what would be found in the underworld. This underworld was divided into twelve representing twelve hours of the night and each of them had different allies or enemies that the pharaoh would encounter. Amduats text would be his guide as to who were his friends upon whom he could call for help and the names of his enemies whom he would need to defeat. The Book of the Dead contains spells to help the King on his way and the Book of Gates would allow him to navigate his way so his soul would not become lost. The texts were all written in hieroglyphic form and the images of humans and animals were left incomplete or were drawn showing them mutilated in order to prevent them from harming the pharaoh on his final journey. You have to admit they certainly had a vibrant imagination. He was originally buried in no fewer than four coffins or sarcophagus, the smallest carved from alabaster and the other three made of granite. The outer two of these were smashed to pieces by grave robbers but the inner two are still in tact with the final granite sarcophagus bearing a likeness of the man himself. We were given only a few minutes of free time here to take in an impossible amount of information before being moved out to make way for the next group. We headed along the floor of the valley and on to the final tomb of Thutmes III trying to keep up with David's brisk pace until we arrived at the entrance. His was one of the first tombs to be built in this valley and he was very well aware of the risk posed by grave robbers and he wished to do all he could to avoid the desecration of his resting place. Secrecy was of paramount importance for him and the location was chosen with great care in one of the most inaccessible spots of the area. The burial chambers themselves were built with corridors and passages at haphazard angles along with fake doors to confuse and disorient any potential thieves. This was the earliest tomb in the valley to have its walls painted and the work was a lot more simplistic than in the other tombs but no less impressive for it. We again had only a few minutes here to take in far more than was possible and then it was time for the tour to end and to begin the short walk back to the tractor that would return us to the valley entrance.

The last visit we would make now before the end of our first week would be to the temple of Hatshepsut which is in the same area as the Valley of the Kings and which is built into the base of el-Qurn. This temple is dedicated to Hatshepsut The Woman Who Was King. The status of women in ancient Egypt was somewhat higher than in any other ancient civilisation but in spite of this the idea that a woman could be King was appalling to the rather conservative Egyptian people. Nonetheless Hatshepsut did become the King and ruled for 15 years. Not just a King either but arguably the first great woman in recorded history easily beating out the likes of Elizabeth I and Cleopatra. She came from a line of strong women including Aahotep who had been a great military leader and had received the 'Golden Flies' which was only issued to soldiers who had shown great courage in battle. Her son Ahmose became Pharaoh and his son Amenhotep succeeded him. This is where is gets a little complicated. Amenhotep left no male heirs when he died so the new Pharoah was a commoner Thutmose who became King by virtue of marrying Amenhoteps sister Nefertiti. He was the guy who erected the two large obelisks at Karnak temple and also began the tradition of being buried at the Valley of the Kings. He did produce three sons and two daughters but by the time of his death only his 12 year old daughter Hatshepsut was still alive. He did however have a son by a minor wife, Thutmose II who became king and who strengthened his claim to the throne by marrying his sister Hatshepsut. She was getting closer to power but wasn't quite there yet and when her husband produced a male child, again called Thutmose, by a harem girl called Isis and proclaimed that this child would be his successor it appeared that this would be the end of her ambitions. Or maybe not. Thutmose II suffered poor health and died after ruling for just 14 years, this left his son who was only a child as King. Because of his young age Hatshepsut (who was both his Aunt and Stepmother, its like a special Royal episode of the Jeremy Kyle show) became his regent and exercised power on his behalf. She used this power to send the boy away from the court, proclaimed herself Pharaoh and used her new powers to make the boy join the army in a remarkable palace coup de tat. Showing remarkable chutzpah she proclaimed that the God Amun had taken the form of her father, visited her mother, and she was the result. She was the daughter of a God and this God even visited her to declare that she was the King and should take possession of the Lands of Egypt. A part of her success is also attributable to the loyalty of key officials within the governing class who were possibly acting out of loyalty and respect for her father. She referred to herself as the 'female falcon' and although she never hid her gender she did dress as a King and even wore a false beard in order to project the right image. By the accounts we were given she was very successful in the role and Egypt flourished. Its economy boomed and trading relationships were expanded. An extensive building program repaired much of the damage that had been done when the Hyksos had invaded. She restored her fathers hall at Karnak Temple, added a chapel and built four great obelisks nearly a 100 feet tall. In spite of all this success however her grip on power weakened as she and her allies aged and unfortunately no one has any idea what happened to her. Its know that her nephew, Thutmose III succeeded her but the events surrounding that succession are a mystery.

What we do know is that a couple of decades after her death Thutmose III had nearly all mention of her removed from all the temples and monuments and replaced her name with his, or her fathers, or her husbands. He obliterated her from history as best he could. At Karnak Temple he had the four mighty obelisks that she had constructed surrounded by mighty walls so that they could no longer be seen from the outside. The irony of this is that the walls offered a lot of protection to them from the deteriorating effect of the weather and they are now some of the best preserved in the country. Her temple was fittingly magnificent, the approach road showing it off to maximum effect against a stunning mountainous backdrop. We strolled around taking a polite interest in some of the smaller artefacts and historical points that we were shown, were led into an area where terrorists had killed some Italian tourists a few years earlier and found ourselves doing a quick reconnoitre to see where the tourist police were and then suddenly time was up and it was all over. That was our last stop on the cruise. From here we would return to Luxor where we would say goodbye to David and the crew, heavily tip the wine waiter and barman who had both done a sterling job and disembark from the ship heading to the hotel that would be home for the next week.

Upon our arrival at the front doors of our new hotel we were greeted with a choice of drinks to refresh ourselves, disappointingly they all turned out to be non-alcoholic but we sipped them politely as we waited for our rooms to be allocated. As we sat and sipped we watched a lady who we presumed was a fellow traveller becoming increasingly frustrated with the hotel porters who were man-handling her evidently fragile luggage. It took reception just long enough to sort our room key that we were able to watch as she reached breaking point and lunged at one of the porters arms outstretched and was then wrestled to the floor by several security guards. This was clearly going to be a change of pace from the previous week. We were shown to our room by a young man eager to pick up a tip and were walked past a large and inviting looking swimming pool with plentiful seating areas to relax in. The pool had two big plusses in its favour;

Number One, We were to find that the water was lovely and warm rather than bollock shrinking cold like most pools in Europe;

Number Two, over the course of the week I only picked up one moderately painful ear infection which soon cleared up after a short course of antibiotics.

Outside of our room was a large enclosed garden, several paths snaking around and through it with two hammocks slung between the numerous palm trees at its centre. The area also contained flower beds around its periphery where there were planted Chrysanthemums, Cornflowers, Red poppies, Iris albicans, Acacia, Dragonwort, Sesban, Papyrus, Jasmine, Lychnis and a whole host of other plants displaying a riot of colour and aromas. However much water supplies may be an issue here it would seem that there is always enough to tend the flower beds. We walked on through the gardens and into the block containing our room which was pleasant and as well as covering the basics (Bed, Bath, Toilet) also had sliding doors on to a balcony where we had a table and chairs which would prove ideal with a bottle of wine in the evening. Shaun attempted to unplug one of the lamps by the bed in order to charge his camera and was mildly taken aback to find that the socket wasn't attached to the wall so as he pulled the plug the socket came with it trailing electrical wire and dust on to the carpet. He shot me a 'what the fuck do I do now' look. I once successfully changed a plug without burning down the house since when all electrical matters are now apparently my responsibility. Contacting reception to complain and requesting someone from maintenance to pop up seemed a sensible choice and I said so. Shaun opted instead to shove it all back in the wall and hope for the best which is probably what the guy from maintenance would have done anyway. We got through our standard hotel room routine quite quickly which consists of six key stages;

1. Looking in every drawer and cupboard,

2. Arguing who gets the one spare pillow which will be in the wardrobe,

3. Lying on the bed to test its comfort,

4. Peering into the darkened bathroom while trying to figure out where the light switch is,

5. playing with all the other light switches to see which one turns on what.

And finally;

6. Standing on the balcony to admire the view and agreeing that "this'll do."

Our holiday has not properly begun until these stages have been completed and as that was now done it was time to start exploring. It was beginning to get quite late in the day and we realised that darkness was close to falling. We had booked only Bed & Breakfast for this second week which gave us the flexibility to dine at the hotel or eat out as the whim took us. Tonight we rather fancied taking a stroll along the bank of the Nile watching the sun sink below the horizon, perhaps not hand in hand as that would get us arrested or beaten up (or possibly both!) until we happened across some charming little eatery that would cater for our every gastronomic whim. The reality of the river front in Luxor during the evening was a long way from this fantasy. There were huge crowds everywhere we turned, every available spot of standing room had someone in it and for many of them we were their centre of attention. People tried to sell us fabrics, watches, refreshments, jewellery, souvenirs, excursions and every third person shouted "Kalesh" trying to get us to take a horse drawn carriage ride around the city. We tried to feign disinterest but to no avail. Shaun even pretended at one point not to speak English and switched to French in an attempt to give the impression that he would definitely be interested in whatever they were selling if only he could understand. This backfired magnificently as the merchant switched into French without missing a beat and continued his sales pitch. Add to this a ridiculous quantity of police milling about shouting at people and driving round at 10m.p.h. with their flashing lights and sirens for no apparent reason and you can see that this evening was falling a long way short of what we had hoped for. Some twenty minutes later the hotel restaurant had become our sanctuary from the bustle outside and we dined on steak and chips washed down with a generous helping of wine purely to numb the disappointment of the evening. We finished off by sitting out on the balcony of our room, enjoying the warmth of the evening, some alcoholic refreshment and each others company, and when you get right down to it, what I ask you could be better than that.

During the cruise we had visited the Valley of the Kings and the Valley of the Queens which had both been spectacular. We were aware that there was a third valley that we had not visited which was the Valley of the Artisans which unfortunately didn't appear on any of the organised excursions from our holiday company. We had arranged to meet up with a couple we had met on the boat, whom I shall call Mike and Jennifer, for a meal at the 'Red Lion Pub' in downtown Luxor and the name had raised our expectations perhaps a little too high. I had been expecting the sort of English themed pubs that are so common on the Costa del Sol but this was not that. From the outside it looked like an abandoned block of flats, possibly because it was, and the only indication that it was even a pub was the battered laminated A4 sign stuck to the front door. On entering there was only one way to go and that was up. A narrow tiled staircase led us up to a small room with six tables each surrounded by unstable plastic chairs of the sort you used to sit on in school, a 'bar' in the corner which was just six feet of kitchen work surface with a single beer pump on it and a bowl of peanuts which positively glistened with the deposited sweat and urine of all the people who had handled them before. There was a total lack of any sort of décor which might indicate that this was a place for enjoying yourself. Where was the blackboard with 'Today's Specials'? Where was the jauntily angled wine rack displaying their selection of vintages? Where was the subdued and subtle lighting creating just the right ambience? It was just plain white walls, plain tile floor and plain plastic tablecloths brightly lit by fluorescent tube. There was only one small window at the end of the room which offered no view. If you had added a few metal bars to it this could easily have doubled for a prison canteen.

Realising that the only available beer was a particularly nasty local brew called Stella which had absolutely nothing to commend it we instead handed over a fistful of notes for a bottle of wine and were issued with a stack of plastic pint glasses from which to drink it. We were also handed the menu which was a piece of laminated white card with the following choices;

Burger & Chips

Cheese Burger & Chips

Chip Butty

Cheesy Chips

This place was in no danger of acquiring a Michelin Star, at least not without some serious blackmail. The printed prices after each of the dishes had been blacked out with marker pen and the prices increased, twice! Considering how little effort it would take to laminate a new piece of card I found myself wondering what else they couldn't be bothered to do properly. Once I had started on my pint of wine though the evening started to improve as they so often do with the addition of alcohol. The four of us perused the menu for all of twenty seconds each and decide to push the boat out with four cheeseburgers and chips in spite of the very generous offer from the waiter to 'stick some scampi in' if we preferred. The meal was fine and arrived promptly, although there isn't a lot that can go wrong with a burger and chips, and they were served in some jaunty plastic baskets of the type that you got in Pubs back home during the 1980's. As the wine flowed and we reminisced about the previous weeks cruise I began to feel well disposed to the world in general and by the time we finished our night and had drawn up plans for some independent exploration it really did feel as though all was right with the world and not even the explosive bowel movement just a few hours later would break my good mood. Up until then I didn't even know it was possible to fart so hard when your crapping that some of it ends up above the toilet seat. You live and learn!

When we rose the next day and got ourselves prepared for our first exploration which would be the valley of the Artisans and we were happy that we had found Mike and Jennifer to go with us. At this point we were both very new to the exploring thing as neither of us had travelled very much in the past, at least not to anywhere exotic. I had once been to Majorca when I was a teenager and Shaun had visited Disneyland in Florida and been on a beach holiday to Portugal. Somehow we felt ill equipped to be negotiating our way around Egypt on our own in spite of our little outing to the Old Cataract Hotel the previous week. Mike and Jennifer on the other hand (who were somewhat our seniors) seemed worldly wise and were happy to attend to the organising which they duly did. Hiring a taxi was Mike's first job which he managed to secure from the front of his hotel. For the sum of just £10 sterling he got us a personal car and driver for the day. A car and driver! For the day! £10. It seems ludicrously cheap as I look back on it but that driver did stay with us all day. Took us wherever we wanted and sat and waited there for as long as we took until we were ready to be taken on to our next location. Back home £10 wouldn't have even covered the petrol we used. He had made a real effort with the inside of the taxi which I was studying as we headed to our first stop. None of the upholstery was visible due to the large amounts of red cloth and wooden beads draped over every bit of available seat. There was a miniature Mosque in pride of place at the centre of the dashboard with various stickers in Arabic stuck either side and we were fully equipped with seatbelts and working windows along with, I can hardly believe it, air conditioning. It would have been worth a tenner just to get a car with air conditioning, something which you would think would be standard in such a hot climate. We arrived at the Valley of the Artisans and exited the car discovering that the derelict building office to our side was in fact a ticket office. This was a single roomed hut, pretty much in the middle of nowhere at the side of the road with a list of prices pinned up beside a window protected by a series of iron bars running horizontally across it. It might have been more effective if the door next to it hadn't been propped open with a handy brick. The prices didn't bare much relation to the actual price we would pay after a little deft negotiation by Mike but on receipt of our tickets we were a little unsure as to where we should go next. The lad slouched on the chair behind the bars pointed up the road towards a cluster of houses on a hill side and seemed pretty confident that this was the destination we wanted. With a shrug we all set off to walk up to the houses which were sat about half a mile away up a relatively gentle climb. As we drew closer to our destination discussing where we were and what the hell was happening we began to find ourselves flanked by a growing number of children between the ages of 5 and 15. They seemed excited to see us and their calls got the attention of two men who up until that point had been having a quiet nap in the shade of one of the houses. They both rose from their seats, adjusting their clothes as they walked towards us, and the leading man introduced himself and asked to see our tickets. Satisfied we were bona fide customers he asked us if we were ready to see the tomb of an artisan and we replied that we most certainly were. He gestured us to follow him and as we walked it was clear that we were heading straight back to his house, one of the many on this hillside, and he explained to us that this was because all the people who lived here were the descendants of tomb robbers. Their families had discovered these tombs at some point in the past and after breaking into them and discovering their vast stores of treasures they decided that the best way to protect their new found wealth was to build their house directly over the entrance. We walked into his house and through his living room and at the back behind a curtain was the entrance to a tomb. It had been stripped bare of its contents but that was no matter as what we would get to see would outclass all that we had seen on the organised tours. The tomb was dark, really dark. As you stared into the entrance you could imagine that you were staring into eternity, your eye unable to focus on anything, unable to make out a floor or walls, unable to pick out any hint of a shadow or variation in the inky blackness. The two of our teenage companions appeared clutching a large mirror each, one positioned outside of the house in the sunshine where he angled his mirror to shine the sun's rays through the living room and down into the tomb and the other standing deep inside the entrance at a T-junction some 20 metres in where his mirror could guide the sun's rays around the corner and down a darkened corridor that ran off at a right angle to the enterance. Our guide and the four of us began to walk into the blackness, heading a further 10 metres or so along this corridor walking carefully and shuffling our feet as we couldn't actually see where we were treading. The sunlight which was being bounced into us illuminated very little outside of one column of light so we advanced with caution. Our guide, Mohammed stopped us here and began to tell us the tale of the Artisan whose last resting place this was. In summary;

1. He was born,

2. He learned a trade,

3. He made some stuff,

4. He died and some people were sad.

The story wasn't up to much but while Mohammed was telling us he used a third mirror that he was carrying to direct the sunlight one last time. He shone the light onto the walls and ceiling around us. There were numerous brightly coloured relief's on every surface. Because this area was off the usual tourist trail and because of the minuscule number of visitors sweating and breathing out carbon dioxide the colours are preserved in a near original state. The brightness is extraordinary. This Valley of the Artisans is known as Deir el-Medina and this was where all of the workmen lived and died who had laboured to create the Valley of the Kings. Instead of monuments glorifying and testifying to the ancient Egyptians morbid fixation with the afterlife here we were seeing a portrait of everyday life. No gods, no curses, no intrigue. Just the story of an ordinary guy going out to work and putting food on the table for his family. The difference in the size and grandeur of the tomb was immediately apparent but we were also to learn that there was a very clear hierarchy after death for what you could take into your tomb. A simple artisan's tomb such as the one was very unlikely to contain any jewels or precious metals. For anyone who was not a part of the royal court the standards they could expect in the afterlife were significantly lower. They may have to contend with being mummified without the embalming process and may even be buried with their organs still inside their bodies! One tomb was found to contain only a simple wooden coffin, a leg of beef, twelve loaves of bread and a beer. We spent a diverting half hour listening to his stories and taking in the brightly coloured walls and ceiling one square foot at a time, for that was all he could light up with his little mirror. The colours themselves are an achievement as you couldn't just pop out to B&Q and find all your paints ready made and ready to go, you would have to make the six pigments they used with an array of techniques and then understand the whole mythology surrounding the meaning of the colours as they were deployed in the art work.

Green - the colour of new life and vegetation

Red - for life and victory

White - purity and possibly omnipotence

Black - death and the night

Yellow - eternal and imperishable (like the sun)

Blue - for water, sky and the Heavens themselves

This is only a rough guide as the full range of their meaning was enormous and could easily fill a book on its own and even then many artists would vary the use for artistic reasons that hadn't any symbolic overtones at all. For example if painting a large herd of animals alternating colours would be used for adjacent creatures simply to clearly distinguish between them and for no other reason. The use of colour could be very straight forward such as The God Osiris having green skin as this alluded to his power over vegetation and Amun would be portrayed in blue highlighting his cosmic connections but it would seem that you only follow the rules unless you have a good artistic reason not to. Even if you did eschew artistic considerations and decided to stick to the mythology some of it was contradictory and could be applied in different ways. The sun could be portrayed as yellow because it is or it could be portrayed as red to recognise its fiery nature. Red could also mean someone who was filled with rage or could also be used as the normal skin tone for Egyptian men. This all meant that a character portrayed in red could be someone who was filled with rage and who was possibly evil or could just be someone who was victorious or could just be a representation of a person with no mythical overtones at all, it all depends on the context. This different usage and meaning is multiple and complex for all six colours and how on earth archaeologists figured out what it all meant is beyond me. The production of the pigments was fascinating in its own right and you wonder how anyone every stumbled across there production techniques. Some were straight forward such as the use of naturally oxidised iron for red, chalk or soft gypsum for white and charcoal or burnt animal bones for black but the others were more complicated. Green and Blue required the creation of a paste which is produced by the mixing of oxides of copper and iron with silica and calcium. The blue colour even if produced correctly was unstable and likely to darken or even change colour as the years pass. Finally Yellow required a method utilising orpiment (arsenic trisulphide) a compound which has since been used in the construction of the de Havilland Firestreak Missile system. Were these discoveries made by people who were trying to do something else or did someone just sit and spend their days mixing stuff together to see what might happen? Our guide unfortunately didn't know the answer to that and didn't even have the decency to lie to us about it.

Abruptly our time was up and we were ushered back out and into the blinding sunshine. We thanked Mohammed for an unexpectedly pleasing tour (you can substitute thanked for tipped as it means the same thing here) and began to head back down the hill to the taxi with a full phalanx of kids escorting us on our way. Back at the taxi we headed for our next stop which was an Alabaster workshop on the west bank of the Nile. Alabaster is a calcite variation of gypsum to give a textbook definition or more simply is a type of limestone that is characterised by swirling patterns of cream and brown, it is often translucent and is ideal for carving into figurines, ornaments, lamp bases and much else. I was most interested in the chess boards on display and spent an instructive hour watching a craftsmen hand carving the pieces of a chess set from differently coloured and patterned Alabaster along with a history of the game of chess which he claimed was invented in Egypt (if you visit India they will tell you that the Indians invented it and in China you'll be told that it was the Chinese) at the end of which I purchased the chess pieces along with a board and a rather attractive red felt covered display case as a souvenir of our day and in one transaction blowing more of our budget than the rest of the holiday put together. Shaun, Mike and Jennifer were all ripped off to varying degrees for assorted bits of tourist tat and each of us clutching a plastic bag full of memories we made our way back to the taxi and asked to be taken back to our hotels so we could be ready for dinner. Our hotel was on the opposite bank of the river and the nearest crossing was a couple of miles in the wrong direction. As we arrived at the bridge we saw our first serious traffic jam. The police had erected barriers across the road where it led on to the bridge and the two lanes were reduced to one as all the cars were filtered neatly to one side for the police to conduct a check on the occupants. Judging by the amount of time it was taking to check each car we were going to be stuck here for a good hour, or we would have been if it weren't for the fact that a Tourist Police officer spotted us sat in the car and waved us straight over into the empty second lane. Within a moment we were waved through the checkpoint and were motoring along at 30mph towards our destination.

"They don't upset the tourists." was our drivers analysis of the situation and he was right. We began to notice that wherever we went the tourist police were intent on making our life easier; clearing away pesky kids, beggars and traders, stopping traffic for coaches, and later that night when our taxi driver hit a cyclist sending him and his bike sprawling into the middle of the carriageway the police were on hand to drag the cyclist and his bike quickly out of the road and wave us on our way with their apologies for the interruption to our evening. The taxi driver who had hit the cyclist seemed unconcerned by the fact that he had knocked someone over or by the fact that his car might be damaged. He simply assured us that everything was fine as he was a 'professional driver'. There is a joke amongst the taxi drivers of Luxor, I know because I heard it several times, where a driver upsets his passengers by jumping a red light and then turns to them, smiles, and says,

"Don't worry, professional driver."

As he drives on he passes straight through another red light to the horror of his passengers without even slowing down.

"Don't worry, professional driver." he repeats with a smile. As he approached the third light however he did slow down and came to a complete stop. This light was green,

"Why have you stopped?" asked his passenger,

"There may be a professional driver coming the other way" he replies.

Many a true word spoken in jest and that joke tells you a lot about the mentality of Egyptian taxi drivers. We did survive the night and for the next three days there would be no need to go anywhere near a taxi as we were heading to Hurghada on the Red Sea coast. We would be travelling a couple of hundred miles by coach to reach the resort and after being picked up at the hotel we were taken to a muster zone where all the coaches and cars that wished to travel to the coast that day were required to meet at 9am. The road is so dangerous that everyone is required to travel together in convoy with the police leading and following and an armed plain clothes officer deployed on every coach as a precaution. This was more than a decade ago now so the people who were hiding out in the desert would only be killing us in order to steal our belongings rather than killing us for ideological reasons. The twenty four hour news cycle ensures that any British tourists killed abroad by terrorists will feed into the sense of national fear and panic whereas being killed by a robber is somewhat less sensational and will warrant a sober thirty second report somewhere near the end of the bulletin. Anyway the journey went off without incident and we had four hours of air conditioned desert watching and iPod listening to reach our destination. Maintaining the utmost vigilance throughout the journey I was most disappointed to reach the other end without seeing any bandits, not even one on horseback up on a ridge somewhere looking down on us in a menacing fashion.

The desert is surprisingly unlike what I expected although my expectations have been heavily shaped by films like Carry on follow that Camel! The desert should consist of a great expanse of rolling sand dunes in all directions, perhaps with a little shimmering mirage on the horizon. There might be the occasional oasis thrown in there with a small still pool of water, a cluster of palm trees to provide shade and a detachment of the French Foreign Legion lounging underneath. The desert that I was looking out on from my air conditioned coach was somewhat different. This was the Eastern Desert, extending from southeast of the Nile delta in the north down into Sudan and from the Nile in the west over to the Red Sea Coast in the east. There are areas of rolling sand as you start your journey from the Nile but after fifty miles or so it merges into the Red Sea Hills, a rugged volcanic mountain chain running from north to south and rising up to over 7000 feet in height. It is dry, but not as dry as you might think as their will still be rainfall and there are extensive wadis here as a result. These are the dry beds of seasonal streams which will turn from dry, dusty and flat into raging torrents of flood waters before you can shout "help". Most of your view will be sandy yellows and reds but in the outcrops and in the cliff faces you will see large patches of gold, blue and green which are the mineral deposits that are so plentiful in this area and which I am sure someone will get around to mining eventually. There are also plants, not many but some, that have adapted to the limited water supply and they are known as xerophytic. There are even halophytic plants which can tolerate the high salt levels which are found in the salt flat areas, so named because they are very flat and contain a lot of salt. These halophytic plants include many that are ideal for camels being both succulent and fibrous.

Sedge with its deep roots hangs on in there in the sandy areas, Tamarisk Trees cluster around the oases (not palm trees, go figure!). Many of the plants go through their germination cycle when the rains come and store their seeds underground during the dry seasons where they sit waiting patiently for the next wet spell to hit. Many of them are flowering plants like the daisy, iris, mustard, milkweed and convolvulus family. Although I didn't get to see it the entire desert floor can go green, covered in a deep carpet of competing flora all trying to make the most of the occasional and precious water. The Bedouin who are a nomadic population have lived here a long time and have found many herbs which they use as seasoning and preservatives for their food as well as washing their hair and giving their clothes a pleasant scent. They even have a 'tooth brush bush' which produces spikes which have traditionally been used to clean their teeth. And here I was thinking its just a load of sand. Shaun had exercised his right to sit next to the window as I had taken the window seat on the last long coach trip so I was relegated to the aisle looking out past him to see the view. His insistence on having the window seat I found odd as he chose to put his head phones on and listen to music as he drifted off to sleep without even glancing in the direction of the view, the drool on his chin glistening in the morning sun as I looked past him and at the ever changing scenery outside.

As we headed into Hurghada and towards our hotel it was pretty unimpressive. Nothing more than a vast expanse of hotels, many half finished, littering the landscape. Hurghada is a relatively new development on the Red Sea coast and it exists first and foremost to cater for tourists. It existed as nothing more than a small fishing settlement from the early 20th century but during the 1980's as the tourist industry began to boom this little town was to boom with it. The sea is ideal for aquatic sports with clear blue warm waters for windsurfers, kite surfers and yachtsmen and the coral reefs and wildlife draw in the snorkelers and divers. The weather is warm all year round with little rain and plenty of sunshine coupled with sandy beaches on which to relax, it is the ideal combination to attract tourists from within Egypt and from abroad. There is little worth talking about here in the town with no notable history and a lot more touristy stuff than usual; hotels, restaurants, bars and nightclubs, Marinas, casinos and golf courses, that type of thing. The coach crawled through empty streets, empty at least by the standards of Luxor, and as we swung up on to the drive of our hotel I awoke Shaun from his slumber with a swift elbow jab to the ribs. The hotel was magnificent, a complex of three buildings with the corridors and staircases all at the back and every single room sporting a balcony with a sea view. Completing our hotel room check list took a little longer than usual due to the fact that their were two light switches for the bathroom neither of which were in the bathroom. And why you may ask ,considering that in this hotel there was a plug socket in the bathroom could you not put the light switch in the bathroom as well. The room we were in was amazing with two very large and spacious double beds each with around fifteen pillows, air conditioning and a dining area both inside the room and out on the balcony. As you stepped out from your rooms the pool area was as grandiose and over the top as anywhere I have ever stayed. A series of swimming pools on different levels all linked with a series of waterways and waterfalls intermingled with seating areas, pool bars, snack bars and sun-loungers. The hotel grounds led straight on to a shockingly bright white sandy beach and crystal clear sea which was painful to look at in the midday sunshine. This was a place that made sunglasses a practical necessity rather than just a fashion accessory. The Coral Reef came right up to the shore and although excursions by boat could be organised all that was needed was some goggles and a snorkel and you could simply walk out and experience them for yourself. We quickly completed our initial tour of the hotel, found the water-sports centre where we purchased some snorkelling gear and headed back to the room to get changed. I opted for my usual baggy swimming shorts and a t-shirt, telling myself that the t-shirt was to prevent sunburn rather than a desire to cover up my saggy man boobs and popped on a pair of camel leather sandals for walking about on the seabed. One of the first and most important things to learn about coral when you are getting up close to it is that it is razor sharp. One of our fellow holiday makers on honeymoon with his wife ran into the sea that first day for some light hearted frolicking and cavorting, brushed his foot against a piece of coral resulting in a large unsightly gash (insert your own joke here!) which saw him packed off to hospital in the first available taxi. He returned many hours later, heavily bandaged and never set foot in the water again. Myself and Shaun headed in with considerably more caution and soon immersed ourselves in this underwater marvel. The Reefs and wildlife of the Red Sea are arguably the most diverse and stunning of anywhere in or around the Indian Ocean and Arabian Sea. With over 200 types of soft and hard corals in its make up Mother Nature has really gone to town with an explosion, indeed a riot of colour, perfectly framed in the clear blue waters. The reefs require warm salt water in order to thrive and here is simply perfect for them. It supports a thriving and diverse eco-system with not only coral but also fish, crinoids, flatworms, mammals, crabs and cephalopods. There are stingrays, scorpion fish, eels, crocodile fish, lionfish, clownfish, puffers, squirrelfish, angelfish, turtles, octopuses, cuttlefish and upwards of a thousand more, far too many to list here. Around a tenth of all these species are only found here and no where else creating a unique spectacle. This reef is over five thousand years old and extends for more than a thousand miles along this shoreline and it isn't alone. There are numerous other reefs that exist offshore and even some atolls if you head all the way down to Sudan but no barrier reefs of the Australian type which most of us are probably more familiar with. The Red Sea is quite isolated relatively speaking with little of the water here being exchanged with the Mediterranean (due to the locks of the Suez Canal) and the Arabian Sea at the other end. This isolation has led to some significant changes in this area that set it apart. I am sure we are all aware of the threat that global warming presents to coral reefs and I have seen several programmes recently discussing the bleaching (death of the corals which turns them white) and the impact on the local eco-systems. In the red sea it turns out that there are two reasons for at least a glimmer of hope. Firstly there is virtually no river or rain water running into the sea making it unusually clear and sediment free which reduces one of the main and most damaging problems that reefs face especially in tropical oceans. Secondly the land nearby is so dry that large and regular dust storms settle on to the sea causing unusually large temperature and salinity changes that aren't experienced in other areas. This ongoing process has led to corals that are remarkably robust and which have developed a level of tolerance to change which other reefs simply don't have. These two positives however may be overwhelmed by the growth in tourism and the resulting urbanisation coupled with poor planning by the local authorities. Declining water quality from the unregulated population explosion along with direct damage from boat anchors and recreational scuba divers are all taking their toll and although there has been a limited response with the establishment of Marine Protected Areas it doesn't go far enough to prevent serious degradation of the reef as a whole. The greatest threat again faced by the natural environment is unregulated and unconstrained human activity that place short term economic outcomes above the long term destruction of our entire planet. That didn't stop me being here however and spending several hours splashing around the corals and trying to sidle up on unsuspecting wildlife trying to get a better look without spooking them. We had a very pleasant day exploring the reefs and had built up quite an appetite for our evening meal which we took outside on a terrace overlooking the sea we had been in just a couple of hours earlier. We feasted on pizza washed down with a bottle of Chianti which I know doesn't seem very Egyptian but after a hard days sight seeing I think we deserved a treat. We retired early luxuriating in a double bed each and spending about an hour trying to organise the pillows of different shapes and sizes that each bed came with and then slept. We only had the morning free the next day as we would then be heading back to Luxor so we opted for a glass bottomed boat trip to take us out over some of the deeper areas of the reef. The views through the crystal clear water down over these cliffs and mountains of coral along with the teeming wildlife is well worth a couple of pounds of anyone's money and it was just a shame that Shaun spent the entire time up on deck being sick in as extravagant a manner as possible. Throwing up should be I think a solitary activity but I was too learn that Shaun in close proximity to a boat will turn it into a spectator sport. The sea wasn't even rough as attested to by the fact that his sick remained perfectly formed in nice little puddles on the surface with just a few clumps sinking down for our fellow passengers to look at through the glass bottom. On returning to the shore he felt a little gentle so we retired to the room for him to have a lie down before packing up our bits and heading back to the coach for the convoy to Luxor. As it turns out it wasn't entirely down to seasickness that Shaun was unwell and within a few hours of our return to the hotel we were both struck down with a bout of gastro-enteritis that would have us both bed bound for the remaining two days of the holiday. Neither of us were capable of moving much beyond the distance from our beds to the bathroom, our curtains were kept closed and I believe someone may have painted a large red cross on the door outside upon hearing the noises emanating from our bathroom. The night before we were due to fly home it reached the point where we would have to summon the hotel doctor. Reception informed us that they could have the Doctor with us inside the hour but there would be a charge of a hundred Egyptian pounds per patient although this would also cover the cost of any medicines prescribed. We got out our wallets and tallied the remains of our holiday spending money. I had only £40 left but Shaun had £102. It seemed to me that the fairest thing to do at this point was to assess who was the sickest and get the treatment for that person. Shaun took the opposing view that it was his money and the doctor would be treating him. I'm afraid that's how our holiday ended. Me hurling my guts up while trying not to shit myself as Shaun was given attentive medical care just a few feet away. We dressed and dragged ourselves to the airport the following morning and I lumbered up on to the plane looking like Patient Zero from every apocalyptic film about an escaped virus ever made. On the plus side the flight attendants spotted my discomfort and moved some passengers from the back row where they made me a nice bed to sleep my way back to England.

That was the end of our first visit to Egypt but was by no means our last. Around three years later we found ourselves on holiday in Cyprus and we spotted an excursion, a one-day excursion, to see the Pyramids at Giza which are in the outskirts of Cairo. We had lost count of the number of people who when being told of our two week cruise and stay in Egypt were amazed to discover that we had not seen the Pyramids. It was £240 each which seemed quite steep for a day trip but after a short discussion we agreed that it was worth it. We saw our travel rep, offered up the money and were issued with our tickets which had the departure time from our hotel highlighted. One in the morning. That seemed terribly early but was no worse than our expected return time of midnight, a full 23 hours later. When they advertise this as a day trip they really mean it. We were clearly going to be up against some serious time pressures this day but the organisation was first class and our arrival into Cairo International Airport was seamless.

Our guide for the day greeted us as we exited the plane and we were whisked straight past all the other waiting tourists at passport control to a gate at the side where a chap in a dark suit held out a black bin liner. Due to our limited time there the Egyptian government had agreed that we could leave our passports at the airport to be processed while we headed out to enjoy our day. I was very impressed with this organisation, as was Shaun, and we both commented on how well organised it all was. It was only a short time later that it occurred to me that I had just thrown my passport into a bin liner because a stranger who had met me off the plane had told me too. The idea of trying to explain this to the British Consulate later in the day was not appealing. It was however completely legitimate and the same chap was waiting for us when we returned later that day with all our passports processed and stamped ready for the return flight. Anyway we were on the coach now and faced a journey of just under 25 miles to reach the Pyramids at Giza and we would be making the journey at rush hour. I should perhaps explain that rush hour in Cairo begins at four in the morning and finishes at ten at night and one of the notable features is that no one does any rushing anywhere. We crawled through the traffic for the next couple of hours staring out the window at pedestrians and cyclists navigating in, around and past us with ease. Many of the local firms use the cyclists to deliver there fresh goods as they can keep moving even when the traffic isn't and I saw various trailers and bags attached to the bikes. There was even a teenager who was cycling while balancing a square board about a metre across on his head on which were stacked several dozen loaves of bread. Arriving at our destination was sudden and without warning. We turned a corner and there they were, larger than life, just at the end of a street. In my head they should be out in the desert somewhere, not stuck right on the edge of the city with the best views of them offered by the seating area of Pizza Hut. As with everything else progress marches on and the human population continues to spread. In spite of their unexpected location the pyramids are still a marvel of engineering that can take your breath away. There original purpose was to allow the dead pharaohs to ascend into heaven which they believed to be amongst the stars, specifically a fixed point in the heavens that was circled by the stars Ursa Major and Ursa Minor, or the indestructibles as they knew them. These stars were always visible to them and the pyramids were constructed to a precise location and orientation and contained a shaft in the internal structure that would face straight into this fixed point in the heavens so that the ascent could take place on the rays of the sun. These were the original Star-gates. We learned of the importance of the stars in Egyptian myth when we travelled to the Sinai Peninsular and we spent an evening out in the desert with some Bedouin people who showed us how to make bread, smoke a hookah and ride a camel. As enjoyable as that all way the best part of our evening with them was the telescope. They had secured a grant from some agency or other that had allowed them to purchase and site a powerful telescope out here in the middle of the desert where there was no light pollution and the night sky visible through it was magnificent. In their presentation they blended fact and myth and wove them together while pointing out areas of interest and allowing us a closer view through the telescope where it helped their story. Giving us the real names of the stars and their location, when they were discovered and who discovered them along with which gods they represented and their place in the story and development of local culture. Discussing the importance of the stars and the myths that surrounded them followed up by a good meal in a tent out in the desert is an excellent way to pass an evening I can assure you.

The colossal effort put in to the Pyramids made them one of the Seven Wonders of the World, or of the ancient world at least and since 1979 the entire area around Giza has been designated a UNESCO World Heritage Site which gives it special status and protection. While there are a number of pyramids on the site we were here to see the big three and especially the biggest of the three known as the Great Pyramid which is the oldest and most northerly. Standing now at just over 450 feet in height with each side of its base being over 750 feet in length it was constructed as the burial chamber for Khufu, the second King of the 4th Dynasty. It can lay claim to be one of the largest buildings ever constructed. Around 23 million blocks of stone were cut for its construction, all from granite, with its internal passages and its external covering being made of limestone. That external covering of limestone is now almost completely gone although it can be seen in places and would have meant that originally the pyramid was smooth on all sides rather than stepped as it is now. Including that casing the original full height would have been over 481 feet. If you were to visit St Paul's Cathedral in London and look upwards to the top of its great dome you would be staring at a point some 100 feet below the top of our Great Pyramid. Depending on the guide you may find different explanations as to how they were built although the most popular explanation was that a series of earth embankments were built in a gentle slope and which increased in height and length as the construction gained height enabling the large blocks to be dragged into position. Clearly once finished the pyramid would have been buried under these embankments and would require digging out again, a mammoth task in its own right. There may have been 100,000 people working on them on a part time basis when there was no work in the fields as told by the Greek historian Herodotus, or you might be told that there were only 20,000 people who lived and worked there permanently as suggested more recently by archaeologists who have studied the remains on the site. The second pyramid built for Khafre is of a similar scale being 471 feet high and 707 feet on each side, and the third for Menkaure was significantly smaller at only 218 feet high and 356 feet along each side. It may be smaller but it is still a significant structure. For comparison Tower bridge in London stands 213 feet high above the Thames River. We were taken to an area off to the side which gave us an ideal photo opportunity taking in the whole of the site and on disembarking the coach we found ourselves in amongst about 300 children who were quite obviously on a school trip. Although we were in awe of the site we were seeing it was entirely clear from the kids facial expressions and body language that 'not the pyramids again!' was a more accurate description of their feelings. On all sides of this viewing area we were surrounded by children begging, unlike the school kids they had clearly fallen through the cracks in the system and were reliant on the generosity of tourists. The small number of tourist police were quite shockingly aggressive towards the kids including throwing rocks at them to chase them away from the tourists. The kids were only acting out of desperation and the police told us they were sent there by their families and told not to return until they had money to put food on the table, their thinking being that children will be viewed more sympathetically and will extract bigger donations. Some of these children used to live here but had found their houses bulldozed and their families moved on in order to provide a better view of the Pyramids. After a hurried few minutes of picture taking we were bundled back on to our coach and driven down in amongst the structures themselves where we had a short time to explore before walking down to the Sphinx. For those of you who don't know this is a giant carving of a creature with the head of a man and the body of a recumbent lion. Standing some 66ft high it stares impassively out and away from the pyramids as it has for several thousand years now. The sphinx was a mythical creature in possession of great power and between the front paws there is a story written of a young prince who fell asleep in the shadow of this creature. He had been hunting all day and became tired and in need of sleep. As he slept he dreamt that the Great Sphinx spoke to him. The sphinx was covered in sand up to its neck and he promised the young prince that if he freed him from the sand he would become the ruler of all Egypt. Unfortunately the rest of the story is gone so you will have to make up your own ending. The sphinx in Egypt was in the main regarded as a guardian of the tombs unlike the sphinx of Greek mythology which would set a riddle for travellers that stumbled across it and would then strangle and eat them if they got it wrong. The sphinx we were staring at would just kill us to protect the temples behind it without playing any mind games first.

The next part of the trip was a visit to a papyrus museum (or a shop as we would call it) where we had a five minute presentation on papyrus which is named for the plant from which it is made. The stalks of the plant would be taken, the leaves removed and then they would be smashed and flattened. These strips of pulpy mess would then be placed into one layer side by side horizontally and then another layer on top vertically and then left to dry out with a weight pressing down on top.

This resulted in
scrolls and which
appearance to it. We
and cheaply faked by u
rapidly decay and given
were going to spend the
definitely completely ge
that we would clearly be
for them. As it happens
ended up paying for a pi
life which is now framed
sits at the bottom of my
room. It is a powerful sy
good luck to its owner. I
off our day in Cairo with

river it was a sight to see. W
the view and stayed out
docked and were wh
last experience of
headed back t
security ch
we were
board
an

with some local entertainment provided. We mopped up
our three course meal, drank a little wine and after a few
minutes of watching the 'entertainment' which was a
whirling dervish we decided to take a stroll on to the deck.
Realistically how long can you watch a man spinning in
circles with a cape for before it becomes repetitive.
Anyway we stepped to find the sun had settled behind the
horizon allowing the darkness to envelop the city and the
sky line against that inky black back drop was stunning.
Brightly lit buildings stood out in sharp contrast to their
background in every direction. The gigantic golden arches
of McDonalds clearly visible on top of one of the taller
buildings in the central district could potentially have
detracted from the ambience but somehow it didn't seem
out of place. This is a bustling commercial hub, the centre
of modern Egypt. Along the shore just a few dozen
metres from us was the well lit river front thronged with
tourists, market traders, traffic, police, horse drawn
carriages, animals, shops, entertainers. All of human life

...m of activity beneath that
...ge point in the middle of the
...We sipped our wine and took in
...there on deck right up until we
...sked away back to the airport. Our
...Cairo was the security or lack of it as we
...o our plane. We found every desk and
...ck point empty, every door was unlocked and
...able to walk unchallenged all the way to our
...ing gate. We saw no one as we traversed the airport
...d most of the lights had been turned off so we found
ourselves following dark corridors with emergency
lighting only and ended up sitting in a darkened room
with our plane just the other side of an open door. It was
nearly twenty minutes later when a security guard
stumbled across us and made us walk back to the entrance
where we had to wait while all the various officials and
police officers manned their checkpoints. When they were
ready we then walked back through the airport a second
time while they conducted the necessary security and
passport checks until we arrived back at our boarding gate
for the second time and finally got our flight back to
Cyprus, leaving Egypt for the last time. We were both
regretting our wine consumption on the cruise and were
thinking that a little snack and possibly a cup of coffee or
two might be a good idea during the flight. Unfortunately
about two minutes after take off we hit turbulence and I
mean real turbulence, not the pansy ass please keep your
seat belt on unless your going to the toilet kind, I mean
gut wrenching, people crying, being sick, praying kind of
turbulence. The cabin crew remained strapped in their
seats for the entire flight. One lady was violently unwell
and her husband asked for more sick bags as hers was
getting full. The cabin crew did not move and surplus sick

bags were passed down the plane passenger to passenger. In amongst the quiet sobbing of my fellow passengers however was one elderly lady who was laughing wildly and greeted every plunge with an;

"oooooooooooh"

"aaaaaaaaaaaaaah", or indeed,

"wheeeeeeeeee!"

The nightmare continued all the way back with no respite until we were coming into land. As it turns out we didn't need the coffee to sober up, near death works just as well.

TUNISIA

We were boarding our flight to Tunisia which is up on the north coast of Africa. It sits on the opposite side of the Mediterranean from Italy and finds itself bordered by Algeria to the west and Libya to the east. Their climate, at least in the northern coastal regions is typically Mediterranean with hot dry summers and moderate but sometimes rainy winters which is perfect for attracting sun seeking European tourists and their spending money. In spite of some highly publicised terrorist attacks and some civil unrest it has been a beacon of stability at least compared to its neighbours and the surrounding region and has remained throughout the Arab spring as one of the few places that Europeans have continued to holiday. They gained their independence from French occupation on the 20th March 1956 and swiftly abolished their monarchy, created a Republic and spent the next 30 years under the rule of Habib Bourguiba, a moderate voice who was surprisingly ahead of his time. As well as creating a working democracy which was secular in nature he also advanced the cause of Women's rights and I cannot overstate how unusual that is. In the laws introduced after independence women were given virtual legal equality with men, polygamy was banned, education became a right for all and a wife could initiate a divorce. Don't get me wrong, by the standards of the U.K. (which aren't perfect) this is not somewhere I would wish to live but compared to its neighbours it was enlightened and it seems laid the foundations for a more stable and prosperous country. The story doesn't finish well for this President though as he became increasingly authoritarian and forced his election as President-for-Life in 1975 which eventually resulted in a coup against him, albeit a peaceful and constitutional coup which does say something about the country's desire for moderation and stability. We were readying ourselves for four hours of flying crammed into our economy class seats when the following happened;

"Excuse me, I'm afraid you can't sit here if your pregnant!" said an Air stewardess in a firm and authoritative manner to the lady in the row in front of ours.

"But I'm not pregnant." came the reply.

The stewardess was momentarily taken aback by this but rallied magnificently,

"I'm so sorry. It's just that dress your wearing…"

We unsuccessfully stifled our laughter but the lady had enough class to rise above it. With that little interlude out of the way and the stewardess walking away contemplating how she had made a bad situation considerably worse we began to taxi for take-off. We hurriedly completed our final preparations which included having a good book to hand, some money in case we fancied a tiny bottle of wine for a full sized price and finally shoving our knees deeply into the back of the seats in front of us so the people in front couldn't recline them.

This journey takes place a good few years ago now before the Arab Spring and multiple terror attacks not only against tourists but against the Tunisian people themselves. This is about the happy memories of the seven days in which we covered nearly a thousand miles on the Mediterranean coastline from Sidi Bou Said through Tunis, Carthage and down to Monastir and then inland to the town of El Djem (where Gladiator was filmed, except it wasn't), Matmata (where Star Wars was filmed) and out into the salt flats of the Sahara Desert. No lazy days on the beach for us (well, not many), we were here for an adventure. But first we needed to find out where we would be staying as for the first time we had booked a holiday that was allocation on arrival. This was the first and last time we ever took this risk but it was cheap and as we were saving to buy a house at the time the cost was a major driver in our decision making. All we knew was that we were going to Tunisia and that we would be staying somewhere that was at least three star. I had never even heard of allocation on arrival until the travel agent had suggested it and rather boringly and against all my expectations the entire process was smooth and hassle free and we found ourselves at a very nice golfing hotel in the town of Port el Kantaoui. At that time this was one of the most popular seaside resorts in the country equipped not only with two 18 hole golf courses and a top class golf club (it's a shame we don't play golf really) but also pristine golden beaches with a clear, warm sea and swaying palm trees to complete the effect. Port el Kantaoui is a purpose built resort dating from the late 1970's that was clean, well maintained, bursting with diversions to keep the holiday makers entertained but which seemed utterly devoid of any history or areas of cultural interest. It is pleasant enough with a picture perfect marina, large central square with an impressive fountain in the middle (especially at night when the water is illuminated in a garish display of colours), restaurants, bars, shops and thousands of happy tourists milling about with little sense of purpose or direction which is exactly how happy tourists should move about. The transport links were good though, the organised tours reasonably priced and the historical attractions of the country plentiful and from its fairly central location this would prove an ideal base for exploring. Upon arrival at the hotel we handed over our passports at the reception desk, completed the appropriate paperwork and were handed the key to our room just as a porter appeared at our sides to show us the way. We followed him through the spacious, airy bar where someone had really gone to town with the marble work, on through a maze of corridors, into a lift for a short ride up to our floor and followed him into our room. He stopped dead. Looked at the double bed and then back at us, the two gentlemen whom he was escorting and then back at the double bed.

"Sorry about this. If you just come back with me to reception we can sort you another room."

"That's fine, we're quite alright here" I replied hoping this wasn't going to get awkward.

"No No," he said "We can sort it out for you, no trouble."

"Honestly we're absolutely fine here" I repeated and just for clarity added,

"there is no need to move us, really." He was clearly about to insist again when his brain caught up.

"Oh… I see…" followed by a small pause,

"Have a good stay and if there is anything I can do for you just call." This was said with a hint of uncertainty but that didn't stop him accepting his tip as he excused himself from the room. That was the closest we ever came to having a problem as two men on our travels in Africa even though homosexuality is illegal over most of the continent. Actually the only time we faced real, in your face discrimination as a gay couple was on a city break to

Dublin in Ireland. They may well have voted for same-sex marriage now but when we visited we were stopped by the night porter as we returned to our hotel who refused to admit us because, and I quote,

"But your two men, and THAT'S a double room." Capitals denote his emphasis. Let me be clear, there was no inappropriate behaviour or indeed behaviour of any kind. We were not kissing or holding hands, simply being two men together at night was sufficient for us to be singled out and left standing on the doorstep of the hotel. Perhaps its unfair to judge a whole country on one incident and perhaps someday we will go back and see but not just yet. Back in Tunisia we unpacked, took in the view from the balcony, spent ten minutes searching through 117 channels on the T.V. in order to find the BBC World Service, briefly pausing on an episode of Midsomer Murders which had been dubbed into French and then got dressed and headed downstairs to book our excursions. The hotel didn't feel overly large although it was well equipped with facilities for the non-golfers amongst us including a heated indoor pool, on-site restaurants and most importantly for golfers and non-golfers alike, a bar. Only a small group of us had arrived together, no more than a dozen people I would have said and moving through the hotel it was clear that it was a long way from full, a feeling that was confirmed as we arrived at the Welcome meeting where there was no lack of seating. The chairs in one corner of the bar area had been arranged into three rows with a little information pamphlet placed neatly into the centre of each seat. We sat through an instructive talk from one of the travel companies employees who gave us the low down on Tunisia, what to expect and what to look out for and proudly informing us that they had forty eight million olive trees in the country, a fact that he recited clearly expecting more of a response from his audience who, I speak for us all, were thoroughly under whelmed. Every African holiday we have been on had an almost identical set of warnings;

1. Beware of pick pockets, buy a money belt.

2. Always agree a price with the taxi driver first.

3. Don't go walking around after dark.

4. Don't drink the water or get it in your eyes.

5. Be careful on the roads, the drivers are insane.

6. Never pay the first price your quoted.

Actually in Tunisia the water is perfectly safe to drink but contained a lot more salts and minerals than we are used to in the U.K. so although you won't contract cholera it can still cause some stomach upsets and general squitiness. The drivers were insane, the taxi drivers open to negotiation and after dark we were always found in a reputable drinking establishment with several dozen other tourists and therefore most unlikely to be mugged or murdered. The warning of impending doom out of the way the meeting progressed to the bit we were waiting for. The organised tours. The more we have travelled the more adventurous and independent we have become but we are still extremely lazy and there is a lot to be said for handing over some money and letting someone else do all the organising. Our host talked us through the available options while a young man from the bar mingled amongst us with a tray containing the smallest glasses of orange juice I have ever seen. No, that's a lie. There was a Bed & Breakfast we once stayed at in Blackpool which did have smaller and this was a reflection on how tight the Scottish owners were. On our second morning their we arrived at breakfast for our 'Full English' consisting of one sausage, one piece of bacon, one egg, one spoonful of baked beans, one tomato and a half slice of fried bread only for me to find as my plate was placed in front of me that there was no tomato! I looked up at our host,

"You didn't eat the tomato yesterday" was all she said as she turned and walked away leaving me open mouthed and speechless. I'm pleased to say the next time we saw here she had developed a toothache which became infected and caused her a great deal of pain for the rest of our stay. Our host here in Tunisia talked us through the selection of trips, cruises, meals and activities in which we could partake and after careful analysis of which were available on what days and what we could afford we ended up planning trips that would take up fully four days of our week the first of which would be leaving the following morning at the ungodly hour of 5am.

We rose on time nursing the kind of hangover that leaves a second heartbeat in your head (the previous night was the first night of the holiday, what else did you expect?) and after a light breakfast boarded our coach for the two hour journey north along the coast, past the capital city of Tunis and on to our stop of Sidi Bou Said, a rather splendid little town of only a little more than five thousand people which hugs the Mediterranean coastline. During the journey our local tour guide, who approximately one third of the coach couldn't hear, repeated all the facts about Tunisia that we had been told at our welcome meeting the day before, finishing with the boast that there was a thriving olive oil industry and that the country has fifty million olive trees. He timed his talk to finish as we arrived at our destination and informed us that this visit would consist entirely of free time for us to explore on our own and take in the views. Watches were synchronised with the clock on the coach and a departure time for us to return was agreed. Setting off up a steep but promising looking street under a now blazing sun and against a backdrop of light blue sky we found this place was beautiful. Every building we could see had its walls painted in brilliant white with all the windows and doors coloured with a deep and luxurious blue. The streets were cobbled and unsuitable for motor traffic which gave it a much more relaxed atmosphere and we noticed that all the benches, railings and litter bins were painted in the same deep blue creating a stunning overall effect. A living piece of artwork no less. The architecture blended together under this single colour scheme making it difficult to tell where one building ended and another began but as you scanned the skyline there was a mix of houses, domes, balconies, archways and towers all interspersed with occasional palm trees providing a little splash of green in counterpoint to the dazzling white. Sauntering along in the cool shade provided by the high walls around us we first saw the flowers. Outside almost every house, on every balcony and in hanging baskets all around were flowers. Every resident had contributed to this festival of colour it seemed and it was easy to see why it was advertised as the most beautiful place in Tunisia. It seemed to us that it may also be the steepest place in Tunisia as every step took us up an incline that left us slightly breathless and looking increasingly flushed. The further we climbed the more we found a definite arts & crafts vibe to the place as all the streets we passed contained lots of little shops, boutiques and craft stores as well as the obligatory souvenir sellers and of course the café's & restaurants. Our guide confidently asserts that the astounding beauty of this town is such that many artists who came to paint it simply took up residence and never left and the Tunisian Tourism website states that the place is an inspiration for people like the famous artist Paul Klee and famous writer Andre Gide, neither of whom I have ever heard of. We had done no research into this place before we came, simply booking it on a whim, and so the surprise when we reached the top of the street was all the more breath taking. Sidi Bou Said is built on a cliff, hugging close to its edge, and as you emerge from the maze of side streets you are rewarded for your climb with a view over the Bay of Tunis. On little terraces, at little café's with their bright blue seats and dark blue parasols you can relax with a drink and look out over the Mediterranean. Directly below you is the Marina with many hundreds of little boats but as you let your eyes roam outwards you see further into the bay and over at the larger vessels plying there maritime trade, and then glance off to the right hand side and take in the skyline of the capital city with the mountains on the far side of the bay finishing off the scene. On a bright summers day with a clear sky its hard to imagine how it could be any more picturesque. We paused here for some time to take refreshments and way too many photos before reluctantly dragging ourselves away as our deadline to return to the coach loomed. We headed back on a different route so we could see a little more of the town and perhaps learn some of its history before leaving. There have been people here in this place for the best part of a thousand years but the town we are looking at today is the result of the great Ottoman empire of the 18th century. The Turkish Governors of Tunis along with their wealthiest citizens built many of the magnificent palaces and other residences here as an escape from city life, shaping its architectural development and providing the framework for its future development. One of those palaces was called Ennejma Ezzahra which was home to one Rodolphe d'Erlanger and has now been converted into a museum in his honour and with good reason. This is the man who painted the town blue & white during the 1920's although the museum focuses far more on his work as a musicologist specialising in Arabic Music, he even wrote a six-volume work on the subject, and much of his former home is now turned over to displays of various musical instruments and also houses the Centre for Arabic and Mediterranean Music. It even has its own concert venue. The music was to be honest of little interest to me but what he had done with the town justified his recognition in its own right in my opinion. Many of his homes original fixtures and fittings have been preserved for posterity but unfortunately much was also lost when the Nazi's occupied the house during the Second World War and began a looting spree followed up by Allied soldiers who distinguished themselves by adding to the damage. A great deal survives though from artwork to furniture and even a treasure-chest which was reputedly owned by Suleiman the Magnificent, one time ruler of the Ottoman Empire. Our time I'm afraid ran out at this point and although there was clearly a great deal more to see we needed to head to our next destination which was the ruins of Carthage, an ancient city which used to exist where Tunis sits now.

Carthage is one of the most famous cities of Antiquity in North Africa. Its power was so great that it even rivalled the power of Rome itself which as it turned out was a bad move on their part. Originally founded in 814-813 B.C. Carthage had proved to be a great power extending its dominion over large parts of Africa and even up into Spain and Sicily challenging the might of the Roman Empire. Perhaps their most famous citizen, although I didn't know he was from here, was Hannibal of elephants across the Alps fame. The son of a Carthaginian General Hamilcar Barcar who in 241 B.C. was defeated by Rome in the first Punic War, Hannibal found himself with his father in Spain at an early age swearing an oath of eternal hostility towards the Romans and to seek revenge for his father's humiliation. Raised with this purpose in mind he quickly established himself as a respected military leader and at the age of 26 was given command of an army and set out to consolidate control of the Iberian Peninsula starting the second Punic War with Rome in the process. He set off from his base in Carthage with 100,000 troops and 37 African elephants, headed across southern France and made his legendary crossing of the Alps emerging into Italy with all 37 of his elephants although only 20,000 of his troops (or possibly not all of his elephants and some more troops depending on which source you read). He spent the next three years inflicting heavy casualties on Rome's military might but without support he never had the capacity to take Rome itself and as a result he was driven back to Carthage and southern Europe once again fell under Roman control. One thing that was never made clear to me was why anyone regarded having these elephants as an advantage in the first place. Everything I have ever read suggests that although they can bring a great deal of death and destruction that is only because they are prone to panic in battle and run back through the people on their own side. Although not deployed against Hannibal as far as I can tell the Romans were well aware that elephants had two major fears which were the sounds of squealing pigs and the sight of fire. Entirely logically therefore they would coat a few dozen pigs with tar and set them alight. The pigs were pretty unhappy about being burnt alive and would squeal frantically while running around in a panic as they tried to escape the flames. The elephants faced with two of their worst fears rolled into one would unfailingly panic and run, routing the elephant battalion. This weakness was known the world over and in Asia straw could be strapped to a Camel and set on fire achieving much the same effect and during the British conquest of India troops would sometimes simply run at the elephants while shouting and firing their weapons which would also startle them into a retreat. It has been recorded that as a result of this tendency to turn tail the elephant's handler, who would be sat on top of it, would keep a large metal chisel to hand which he could drive into the skull of the beast at the first sign of panic to kill it stone dead and prevent the wholesale slaughter of his colleagues. In the circumstances this seems eminently sensible. As both African and Asian elephants were used for battle I found myself wondering which of them would win if pitched against each other. There is only one reference I could find about combat between African and Indian elephants which is in an account by a Greek historian name Polybius, written some 70 years after the event its veracity is perhaps in some doubt. In it he tells of a battle between 73 African elephants of Ptolemy IV of Egypt and 102 Asian elephants of Antiochus III from the Kingdom of Seleucid. According to Polybius the African elephants again distinguished themselves by looking at the smaller Asian elephants, taking a dislike to their loudness, smell and general demeanour, and turned away from the battle. It seems there only sensible use is to look imposing and intimidate your enemies into submission without the need to fight a battle.

Anyway, even after their defeat in Europe and being driven back to their territories in North Africa Carthage quickly revived with its population, military and economic strength growing rapidly, so strong was this growth that the Roman emissary Porcius Cato the Elder who visited urged in every speech he gave afterwards that,

"Delenda est Carthago",

or Carthage must be destroyed and In 149 B.C. Carthage declared war on Massinissa giving the Romans an excellent reason to destroy it. After three years of resistance Carthage fell and Roman soldiers were let loose to burn and pillage, even sprinkling salt over all the soil so the land would be infertile and when the work was done the whole area was dedicated to the infernal gods and all human habitation was forbidden. This didn't last for long and it was revived and re-built by the Romans a quarter of a century later before being destroyed again by the Arabs in the 7th century and now some 1200 years later the area is just an affluent suburb of the City of Tunis. Enough ruins are preserved here to make it a worthwhile tourist destination and we would be visiting two of them which were the Baths of Antoninus Pius and the archaeological park to which it is attached and the ruins of the Harbour where the great and feared Navy of Carthage was moored. The baths were first and on arrival we headed down into what is left of the basement of this once vast complex, a basement which is now open to the skies above I should add. These are the baths of Antoninus Pius and outside of Rome these were the largest Baths in the world occupying a space of nearly two hectares. Built in the 2nd century and restored in the 4th century they subsequently collapsed as a result of poor design rather than neglect and were used as a quarry for building stone after that. All that remains now are the walls of the basement area, but that still gives you an idea of the size of the place and the setting for the many activities that the baths encompassed. Most Roman baths had multiple pools which varied in temperature, a steam room, places for eating, gambling, needlework, possibly minor medical procedures such as dental work and of course shared spaces for defecation. Toilet time was a communal event and the toilets here were in a semi-circular layout with no dividers to protect your modesty. It was simply a seating area with holes cut out for you to sit over and under each of these holes was a channel of flowing water which would carry away your bodily waste. To my surprise our guide explained that the water did not flow away behind you or even under the seats, all the waste would flow forwards, visible to all as it passed through the middle of the room before following the channel outside and away. I honestly don't think that I could sustain a conversation with another man as one of his turds floated past my feet and worse still how do you look someone in the eye if they are doing a 'head-shaker' and they are getting all flushed and rosy-cheeked?

While the Public Baths here in Tunisia were huge the size and design of these buildings would greatly vary across the Roman world, including not just the Public Baths for the general population but also some very opulent private baths in the Villas of the very rich who didn't mix with ordinary folk. Regardless of their size and location all of them would be based around three primary rooms, the Tepidarium, Calarium and Frigidarium. After removing your clothing in the changing rooms you would first move through to the Tepidarium, a warm room where you would unwind and relax, letting the stresses of the day drift away. Once suitably unwound you move through into the Calarium which is the steam room. The high temperature in here would make you sweat which is supposedly great for getting all the dirt out of your pores. Once you were nice and sweaty and all your dirt had been steamed loose you moved on to an intermediate area where a slave would use a curved knife called a strigil to scrape all the sweat and dirt off you and then once cleaned you jumped into the Frigidarium which is exactly what it sounds like, a cold bath. Although this was a social event from start to finish there would be no intermingling between the sexes and men and women would have their own separate rooms or in the smaller bath houses there would be different times of the day allocated to each gender. Thinking of it in today's terms it's much more like a health spa than a swimming pool and if you're interested and want to see one for real there is no need to even leave the country. The Romans built a great many bath houses in the U.K. many of which are still well-preserved today such as in Bath where there is a museum on the subject as well. I might also recommend the ruins at Welwyn Hatfield which have the added attraction of being preserved in a steel vault under the A1(M) motorway near the central roundabout of the Welwyn By-Pass. There can't be many two-thousand-year-old ruins preserved in such an unusual location nor who's entrance is more reminiscent of a nuclear bunker than an archaeological site.

Our visit to the Baths over we headed out for a short walk through the adjacent archaeological park which was pretty enough but who's only really notable features were the remains of some cannon balls heaped up in a pile which had little connection with the area and the outline of the grid system of roads that would have typified the Roman settlements of the time. Our short walk concluded it was time to move on.

The location of Carthage helped in making it a maritime power to be reckoned with. Any ship that wished to sail through the Mediterranean would have to pass through the relatively narrow sea passage between Carthage and Sicily and this strategic naval advantage enabled them to exert great influence far beyond their shores. This focus on maritime power led to the construction of two very large artificial harbours within the city itself. One was to service the fleets that plied their mercantile trade across the known world bringing enormous wealth, knowledge and goods to the people and the other was to accommodate the 220 ship navy of this city state. A single walled tower stood watch over these two great harbours that were so vital to their interests. For three hundred years before the Punic Wars the Cathaginian navy had dominated its sea lanes and was renowned for its seamanship, quality and innovation of design. The demand for ships was so high that they even developed a process of mass production where the individual components were produced in quantity and then transported to the docks where they could be quickly and easily assembled into warships as required, quite an achievement that pre-dates mass production in England by near two millennia. These warships could be powered by both Sail and Oar dependent not only on the weather conditions but also whether they were in battle. If you're fighting its preferable to have the control and predictability of the Oar powered motion rather than having your sails up and relying on the wind. Control of direction and speed were vital because the main tactic in naval battles of the time was to ram your opponents amid-ships with a large bronze battering ram that was mounted below the water line at the prow. The oarsmen could give a ship a top speed of 8 knots in any direction which the wind could not be relied on to do and they could also slow down before the impact so as not to bury their ship too deeply in the enemy's hull which might result in them getting stuck. As well as fighting naval battles the fleet was used for multiple other roles such as blockading enemy ports, raiding supply ships, transporting armies and keeping the troops supplied once you had taken them where you wanted them. The great harbour for the warships, or at least the ruins of it you can now see show a great circular design over 300 metres in diameter and around 2 metres deep with an entrance over 20 metres wide. There was an island in the middle which had a capacity to dock 30 ships and also housed the large Admirals tower which oversaw both harbours. Around the outer ring were roofed sheds, each of them around 40 metres long and 6 meters wide which could hold another 170 ships. The entire thing was surrounded by massive fortified walls and had facilities to bring in infantry and chariots for rapid boarding. There is a complete record of what was here, how it looked and how it was used and if you have a good guide talking you through it you can use your imagination to rebuild it in your mind's eye from the foundation stones around you.

With that our first day's tour was completed and it was time to return to our hotel. Returning to our room we peeled off our clothing and began the process of removing the layers of dirt we had accumulated during the day. I also needed to apply some soothing cream to some bits of sore skin. As anyone who is carrying a bit of extra weight can appreciate hot weather and walking can combine to produce some seriously painful chaffing around your nether regions. There was one hot summer back in England when I worked at a supermarket with useless air-conditioning where the chaffing became something of an issue. Scouring the shelves for a solution the only thing to be found which promised some relief was a jar of Vaseline which I duly purchased. Retiring to the staff toilets for privacy I dropped my trousers and using my index finger began applying the Vaseline to my now red raw skin, around and including the very hard to reach parts round the back! Having finished I thoroughly washed my hands and headed to the staff room where I placed my little tub of Vaseline on top of my locker and then left for the canteen to have some lunch. Finishing my break and heading back on to the shop floor feeling much more comfortable than before I thought no more about my little tub of Vaseline until my return to the staff room at the end of my shift. Entering the room I discovered my manager holding my little tub of Vaseline, dipping his finger into its contents and carefully dabbing the substance on to his dry, cracked lips;

"I just borrowed some of this, I hope you don't mind."

It took me a second to gather myself and wasn't sure how to respond but telling my Boss he was dabbing a combination of Vaseline and sweaty ass juice on his lips didn't seem like a good idea.

"No problem" was all I managed before walking out and laughing to myself for the entire journey home. With that memory in mind and laughing to myself again we headed out to finish our day with dinner and a few drinks at the pool bar before retiring for a good night's sleep. We had another busy day coming up tomorrow.

Although we had booked organised excursions we were also growing in confidence as travelers and as today was a free day we decided to head off on our own to visit the town of Monastir which was some 30 miles south from where we were staying. We had sought some advice from our holiday rep at the hotel about getting there and she had suggested using the railways which were relatively cheap, safe and reliable and so it was that we found ourselves in the booking hall of the local station. Keep in mind that this in an Arabic country that speaks French and you will not be surprised that nobody at the station spoke any English. So often when we travel abroad we are cocooned in a little English bubble surrounded by people who have chosen to work in the tourist industry and who's C.V. will include the line; fluent in English. When you feel a bit adventurous and go off the beaten track, leaving behind your guides and purpose-built facilities you can suddenly find a pretty big language barrier in the way just as we did today. We waited patiently for the people in front of us to make their purchases and it was our turn to step forward and make a purchase of our own;

"two return tickets to Monastir please." I said mustering what should have been a friendly expression but which came across as desperately hopeful. I received a mumbled response accompanied by a shrug of the shoulders from the chap behind the glass who then gave me a 'yeah, what now?' kind of look. Responding to this in time-honoured fashion my voice was raised slightly and my words were more slowly and deliberately formed as they left my mouth, all the better to help him understand. Another shrug of the shoulders from my unhelpful friend across the counter indicated that this approach was not going to get me anywhere. Not wishing to admit defeat and determined to get to my destination I fell back on plan B which consisted of opening my guidebook, pointing to Monastir on the map contained within and with a no-nonsense 'don't fuck me about' tone in my voice said,

"two tickets, TWO TICKETS" while waving two fingers at him. The son of a bitch did no more than look me straight in the eye and in perfect crisp English replied;

"next counter". and pointed to the guy sitting next to him. Giving him a look of my own myself and Shaun shuffled over to join the adjacent queue, waited patiently and on getting to the front immediately presented the open guide book and did the whole shouty pointing routine again. He looked at me and replied;

"Certainly Sir, singles or returns". Caught off guard by his fluent response it took me a moment to reply that I wanted returns and he nodded and printed two tickets. He then pointed at the price on the ticket, I parted with a small bundle of notes, received our tickets and we were on our way to the platform.

The platform wasn't a platform but a pavement alongside which the trains would stop and you would have to climb up into the carriage, disabled access being not remotely possible, and inside we found less than a dozen seats. The approach was very much standing room only so as to maximise the volume of passengers that could be carried, not that we would be standing on the train for long as at the first station we reached we had to change trains and then again at the next station. Two changes of train to cover the 30 miles to Monastir seemed a little excessive and we never got an explanation of whether this was a normal occurrence and part of the plan or down to exceptional circumstances like a breakdown, engineering works or possibly sand on the line. There is another possible explanation as well. Although there is one national rail network under the control of SNCFT the tracks themselves were built in a piecemeal approach involving British, French and Italian companies and perhaps most impressively they used different gauge tracks in different parts of the country necessitating a change of train wherever the track gauge no longer matches. After a mere hour and forty-five minutes we arrived in Monastir and stepped off the train, blinking under the assault of a blinding midday sun and stepped out to explore this beautiful little coastal town. A Mediterranean climate that is more moderate than the inland parts of the country, hot summers, mild winters, sunshine and little rainfall had made this a thriving centre for tourism. Monastir was the birthplace of the former President Habib Bourguiba who was mentioned earlier and his mausoleum is located here. The town has produced a couple of Prime Ministers and several famous footballers who I honestly couldn't name now as to be honest, I didn't really care. The streets were bustling, the people friendly and the sights agreeable but all that was just the appertiser. Our main reason for coming here... that's not true, my reason for coming here and dragging Shaun along with me was to see the Ribat. This is the ruin of an Arab fortification that was built for the defence of Islam back in the 8th century but is now more famous for its starring role in Monty Python's Life of Brian where it doubled up as the Holy Land (which it also did in the series Jesus of Nazareth). The Islamic empire that had spread across North Africa sought to protect itself from the heathen people to the North and coastal defences such as this were built stretching over many thousands of miles. At its most potent this particular fort was home to more than 30 canon, high heavily fortified walls, a high tower for reconnaissance of the sea and surrounding land and a labyrinth or corridors, rooms, staircases and battlements. It wasn't just for show and saw action in the 15th and 16th centuries with part of it even being destroyed by the Spanish Navy in 1550. Still it survived and thrived becoming a well-known religious education centre and even a place of pilgrimage for the faithful. During the 1960's when this was the President's home town and this was the main attraction extensive renovations were undertaken and it was in this greatly improved state that the Monty Python team descended. The six cast members played forty different roles and created a film that caused uproar for its blasphemous interpretation of the bible story. For those who don't know it's about a boy called Brian who is born at the same time as and is mistaken for Jesus. Pretty much every branch of Christianity came together to condemn the film and John Cleese even joked that they had succeeded in uniting them all for the first time in two millennia. So outraged were some people that the film was banned in many places which greatly added to its appeal and made it even more successful. Norway banned it for a year leading to a marketing campaign in Sweden where it was sold as 'The film that is so funny that it was banned in Norway.' This ban only lasted for a year after their politicians realised that they just needed to grow up unlike Ireland who kept their ban in place until 1987, eight years after the film was released! For sheer determination to stick to their guns however the prize must go to Torbay Council in Devon and the town of Aberystwyth in Wales. It was only in the latter half of 2008 that Torbay finally lifted its local ban and allowed cinemas to show the film leaving Aberystwyth alone as the most backward place in mainland Britain. It was only when one of the original cast members of the film Sue Jones-Davies was elected Mayor in 2009 that the ban was lifted and the film was finally allowed to be shown. Such was the sensitivity of the topic that the Monty Python team even had trouble with the production of the film as it was originally to have been financed by E.M.I. who pulled out when they saw the full script and considered it to be blasphemous. As fortune would have it George Harrison, of Beatles fame, stepped in, mortgaged his house in London and stumped up the millions of pounds needed to keep the production going. When asked why he replied;

"Because I wanted to see it."

Eric Idle said it was the highest price ever paid for a cinema ticket. The team had written the film while sunning themselves in the Caribbean and apparently regard it as the best writing they had ever done and I am inclined to agree, and for that reason I was experiencing my usual childlike excitement as we reached the sea front and the Ribat came in to view. The camera was put to work and we began a circuit of the exterior until we came upon a small entrance where for a small fee you can gain entry and explore its corridors and courtyards for yourself. If you are a big fan of the Life of Brian then you may with some effort even be able to work out where some of the scenes were filmed but not easily as none of the information or displays in the place ever mention the film, its time as a film set has been whitewashed from its history which I think is a terrible shame. Without that film we, and many other visitors I'm sure, would not have gone there in the first place. For such a relatively small building its impressive what could be achieved with some set dressing and a bit of paint. Market places, residential streets, courtyards, palaces, and all in an area you can walk across in less than a minute. When you compare what the place looks like and was then made to look like you have to respect the skills of the workmen behind it. What looks in the films like ancient pillars and balconies were nothing more than an illusion and it made it exceptionally difficult to be sure of what I was looking at. I guess that's the magic of film at work. Shaun trudged along behind me as I bounded around staring into corners and up at staircases with my head tilted at a thoughtful angle before confidently asserting;

"yes, this is where they did the bit about..." with Shaun issuing stock responses such as,

"really",

"well", and

"never" but not for one moment dampening my enthusiasm. As well as the Life of Brian and the Jesus of Nazareth mini-series there have been many other films that have used locations in Tunisia, perhaps most famously Star Wars, The English Patient, 1001 nights and Raiders of the Lost Ark. Indiana Jones has scenes filmed in Sedala, Sousse, Kairouan and Sidi Bouhlel. These towns doubled up as Cairo even though the architectural style is absolutely nothing like Cairo although they at least made the effort to remove nearly 400 T.V. aerials from Kairouan when they filmed the skyline sequence. If you feel so inclined and have the time you can even visit the Avenue 5 Novembre where Harrison Ford famously shot dead the swordsman and where the Nazi's chase Marion down the street. I am sure that I cannot have been the only tourist that day who was more excited by the

Hollywood connection and these little stories than by the ancient history of the place. The film industry was mostly a big plus for the country but it could occasionally cause some unexpected problems. When Star Wars was being filmed here a large prop was created of a military vehicle called a Jawa sand-crawler which was left close enough to the Libyan border that it received a response from the Libyans. They threatened Tunisia with mobilisation of their military if this 'threat' wasn't removed. The Authorities had to contact George Lucas and get him to re-site it to avoid a diplomatic and possibly military incident.

Having eventually dragged Shaun around every conceivable nook and cranny down below the only place left to go was up the tower where Brian had fallen off and landed in a spaceship. Emerging from the stone spiral staircase, slightly breathless, the view of the city from the top was one to savour and it gave us an excuse to stop and get our breath back. Sometimes you have to stop, sit down and enjoy a moment of quite reflection to really appreciate something, after all, it might be the last time that you are ever in this place. The tower stands well above the rest of the building and above most of the surrounding town, including the Mosque which is adjacent, granting stunning vista's in all directions. During these few minutes we shared the space with an Australian chap who it turns out was circumnavigating the globe. He had set off from home in Melbourne a couple of months before and travelled eastward eventually finding himself here. We chatted for some time up there, me taking the opportunity to chat to the only circumnavigator I have ever met about his adventure and interrogating him about the cost and the planning involved which was daunting to say the least. I kept this up until he made his excuses and headed on his way which is when Shaun who was still taking in the views asked if we were ready to head off. Taking the hint and deciding to be prepared I rummaged through my pockets for the rail tickets as we headed back towards the station. It was then that I discovered we had been sold singles in spite of my clear request for returns.

"Good grief" I said aloud. Well… it may have been a little earthier than that but you get my meaning. Bracing myself for Shaun's reaction to the news it was a relief when instead of bollocking me he was pleased at the opportunity not to use the train again;

"let's just get a taxi, it'll take us straight back to the hotel" which was true and so we flagged down a taxi, negotiated our price in advance and settled into air-conditioned comfort for a half hour drive to the hotel. We found ourselves in a Japanese Car, with a French speaking Tunisian driver, listening to a British pop song on an American radio speeding along a brand-new road back to our hotel. We were experiencing Globalisation in action. Our early return to the hotel was welcome as it gave me time to have a little nap to re-charge my batteries while Shaun sat out on the balcony and read his book before heading out for an evening on the town. It was a very pleasant place in the early evening, comfortably cool with the light fading and becoming softer, taking the edge of the all surrounding glare you experience when the sun is at its highest. With throngs of people filling up the streets, bars and restaurants both in the centre and stretching down to the marina were beginning to fill or at least looked like they were as the waiters sat all their guests in the most visible places to give the impression that there was an ambience inside. We had made an effort that night before heading out with me going the full Marks & Spencer's again, Chinos and a light blue plain cotton shirt with smart black shoes and Shaun opting for a pair of designer jeans, smart brown shoes and a light red patterned cotton shirt. Shaun always gets dressed after me now because I apparently cannot be trusted in coordinating our sartorial choices. There are a whole word of rules which I confess I'm not even close to understanding when it comes to dressing as a couple. There have been so many times over the years where Shaun has dressed for an evening out in what he thinks are perfectly appropriate clothes but on seeing my choices announces that he can no longer wear what he has chosen. His objections seem to fall into three main themes;

1. I am too smart and he now looks scruffy.

2. I am too casual and he now looks too smart.

3. I am dressed in too similar a style and it

"just looks weird."

We had our night out and for once our excessive food and drink wasn't a problem as the next day was free of commitments. A lazy day. A pool day. A day without breakfast because we slept in too late. That was fortunate as it meant we were refreshed for an exhausting two-day trip into the countries interior which would begin the following morning.

We weren't leaving till 8am but we still rose early as we hadn't done any packing for the overnight stay and we wanted to shower and eat a leisurely breakfast before setting off. We knew that the first part of the day would be hours on a coach, collecting other guests from hotel's around the resort and then driving south to the town of el Djem where our tour was to commence properly.

6.00am and the alarm call from reception came through which consisted of an automated and rather posh female voice informing me that this was an alarm call and it was time to wake up. It then presented me with two options; Press 1 to switch the alarm off or Press 2 to snooze. There is only one sensible choice and I pressed the two. 6.02am and the phone rang again. It was the posh automated voice again informing me that this way my morning alarm call and giving me my options again. Two minutes, two bloody minutes after the first call, what the hell kind of a snooze is that I ask you. Faced with the choice of repeating this every two minutes or just getting up, I got up. Shaun had actually roused himself at the first alarm call and was already occupying the bathroom so I threw a change of clothes, my book and iPod into my rucksack by which time the bathroom was free. At 6.20am we had both showered and packed and realised that we could have easily had another hour in bed and still be ready in plenty of time, instead we now had forty minutes to kill until breakfast would be served. Having forgotten which channel the BBC World service was on I again scrolled through the 117 available, pausing on the same episode of Le Midsomer Meurtre, and then looking crestfallen as I found the right channel and discovered that the sports news was on. There are plenty of dedicated sports channels so quite why we need to have sports on the news channel is beyond me. I opted instead for the American news channel CNN who were covering a shooting in the United States. In case you have never watched them this is all any American news channel ever covers They were interviewing some asshole who was explaining how in his opinion the problem of guns could only be overcome by having more guns. I came very close to sustaining a serious eye rolling injury at this point but I was at least relieved not to be listening to the inane drivel that is football commentary. And this was how I passed the time until breakfast after which we joined our coach for the long trip down to the town of el Djem.

The town itself is unremarkable, small, with limited opportunities for refreshment or tourist tat purchases but the one thing that it does have is a Roman Amphitheatre, and one of the best preserved Roman Amphitheatres outside of Rome at that. It was built in the third century which means it is the better part of two thousand years old making its current condition all the more remarkable. It is in fact the third one to be built in the area, an area that was originally known as Thysdrus, with the sizes being upgraded to accommodate more and more people, from around five thousand in the first construction to eight thousand in the second and then a massive jump to thirty thousand in the third. There are some limited remains still visible of the original two which are only a short distance away from the museum but they are unremarkable, at least in comparison to the well preserved third arena. This may well have been the last of these constructions anywhere in the Roman Empire although I am basing that on the word of our guide who also told us that the film Gladiator was filmed here, which it turns out it wasn't. The Gladiator lie is repeated regularly even though on the locations given at the end of the film itself and even on the IMDB website, Tunisia is never given as a filming location. There was one internet source I found that suggested a CGI version of el Djem may have been used but I found it impossible to get that verified by a trusted source. The amphitheatre is no less impressive for having this lie attached and if you ever visit you will find that it is visible before you enter the town and does dominate the skyline, nothing else here comes close to matching either its height of volume. Indeed, that is deliberate as the construction of buildings within the immediate area is tightly controlled with limits on the height and style of any developments restricted by law and subject to review by the local authorities as well as the National Heritage Institute (who do the science and preservation) and the Agency for the Presentation of Heritage and Cultural Promotion (who figure out how to exploit it for maximum commercial advantage). We had driven in silence for most of the morning but as we drew close to our first stop our guide rose from his seat and began to talk to us about our trip. He regurgitated the usual facts about the country's population, industry, history and of course the fact that there were now fifty-two million olive trees in the country and that this was a very major industry for them. He explained the plans for our next two days with him, where we would be travelling, what we would be seeing and where and when we would eat and sleep. He timed his speech perfectly and began discussing our first stop at this ancient Roman Arena just as the ancient Roman Arena came into view. As soon as it was visible we all began frantically searching for our cameras in order to take piss poor photos through the moving coach window. We drove up to and parked in the shadow of this place. The impressive architectural façade in front of us contains three levels of arcades for seating the audience of thirty or maybe thirty-five thousand spectators. It is constructed entirely of stone blocks, has no foundations and most unusually is free standing rather than built against a hillside. Normally the seating would rise upwards carved out of an already existing hill but here it is entirely artificial with the tiers supported by a complex system of arches modelled on, but not an exact copy of, the Coliseum in Rome. The level of preservation here is surprising for its age with the external walls, its underground passages and the arena itself in excellent condition. At least the stone parts are anyway, a large part of the underground area in the oval shaped arena has been exposed as the wood roof of the tunnels which was also the floor of the arena has rotted, collapsed and disappeared over the centuries. Within the oval area there is now a large oblong hole which stretches most of its width allowing you to glance down to where the gladiators, animals and prisoners would have been before emerging to put on their show. The tiers of seats have been most badly damaged by the passage of time and although recognisable in places are unsafe and closed off to the public. That has led the authorities to restore the seats to their former glory in just one section so that visitors can now see them and walk upon them to get a sense of what the Roman citizens were experiencing. It has to be said that what they were experiencing was spectacularly brutal.

Hail, Caesar, Those about to die Salute thee.

Or

Ave Imperator, morituri te saluting

Those who were about to die and doing the saluting were professional gladiators, Christians and condemned prisoners as well as a healthy selection of wild animals for a bit of variety. The job of these games was very simple, to provide entertainment to the masses by fighting with great skill and courage and then to kill or be killed at the end. Originally the games were associated with funerals, the writer Tertullian during the 3rd century B.C. discusses the belief that the spilling of blood at a funeral would allow the soul of the deceased to find favour with the Gods. Originally the family would sacrifice slaves who they considered of little value or prisoners of war perhaps until two brothers decided to liven things up by bringing in gladiators to their father's funeral. Starting small with just three pairs of gladiators it proved to be an astounding success and the size of the games and the brutality of the contests grew with time culminating in 65 B.C. when Julius Ceasar paid tribute to his father with funeral games comprising 640 participants as well as an assortment of wild animals. Some twenty years later he arranged another set of funeral games in memory of his dead daughter and to simultaneously celebrate his recent great victories in Gaul (France) and Egypt. This was part of the development away from being just a funeral right to becoming mainstream entertainment to the masses with their size and brutality on a seemingly exponential growth path. People who were already half dead from starvation and torture were thrown out to be torn apart by wild dogs, whole families were sent in to be hacked apart or clubbed to death by the professional gladiators. One Emperor by the name of Domitian was so incensed when a member of the crowd jeered his favourite gladiator that he had the man dragged from the stands and thrown to a pack of wild dogs who duly tore him limb from limb. The crowd loved it. No act of depravity of brutality seemed to cross a line for these people and the floor where they fought was kept covered in sand to absorb all the blood that would be spilt. For those who were fighting their survival wasn't even to be determined by their own prowess but by the whim of the crowd that they were entertaining. Even in defeat with a cry of 'Habet Hoc Habet' (he's had it) a contestant may still find salvation in the audience if they had been entertained by his efforts. The crowd would indicate their feeling with a gesture of the thumbs. Flicking their thumbs away from the body, a thumb's down as we would term it, the crowd would be making it clear that they wished a death to occur, but pointing the thumbs inwards towards the body, or a thumbs up, indicated that they had been mightily entertained and even though the gladiator had lost he should be allowed to live and fight another day. Alternately the winning gladiator who has vanquished his foe may find that the crowd has decided he wasn't sufficiently entertaining and with the simple gesture of their thumbs a man dressed as the Ferryman of the Underworld would step forward and kill the poor chap anyway. The combatants may have been prisoners, foreigners, Christians or a fellow gladiator but it may also have been an animal and the more exotic the animal the better. Bulls, wolves, bears, wild boar, buffalos, tigers, leopards, hyenas, elephants as wells as the lions we all expect were used for the entertainment of the people. Such was the fear of facing these creatures unarmed many chose suicide instead. Our guide recounted the tale of two dozen prisoners who strangled each other to death rather than face the arena, although he didn't seem to know what the last one left would have done. If a weapon was available then stabbing yourself in the chest or in the throat was an option or maybe slitting open the veins in your ankles as well as your wrists just to be sure. In desperation you may even get inventive like the prisoner who killed himself with the only thing that came to hand… an excrement covered sponge. This was to be found in the toilet and was available to everyone to clean their backside after a bowel movement and rather than face a prolonged and exotic death out in the arena he thought it better to force the sponge down his throat until it got stuck and choked him to death. That someone could be so desperate surely highlights the terror that all the participants must have faced in the hours before their turn would come. This brutality continued for another four hundred years until the surprisingly exact date of January 1st 404 A.D. when it was suddenly and quite unexpectedly outlawed. By this time Christianity had become the official religion of Rome but seemingly had no problem with the sadism of the games until a Monk named Telemachus stepped in. Visiting from the East he was so appalled by the violence that was happening right before his eyes that he ran forward into the fight, inserted himself between the sparring gladiators and tried to separate them. The crowd were somewhat unimpressed with this and stoned him to death on the spot. News of this quickly reached the Emperor of the day, Honorius, who was so disturbed by this treatment of a holy man that he banned the games immediately and that was that, they were never held again.

We were given a little free time to explore the place once our guide had finished his blood and gore fest and after an hour of wandering aimlessly we returned to the coach and were whisked off to the next part of our tour. This was the camel ride in the Sahara. The image I have in my head of the Sahara is of a vast expanse of sand with rolling dunes as far as the eye can see and I'm pleased to say that the location picked for our camel ride matched that expectation, but it needn't have. It is the largest hot desert in the world (The arctic and Antarctic are cold deserts and are much larger) and most of it is barren, hard and rocky. It spreads from the Atlantic coast of Africa in the east to the Red Sea in the west. To the north it is bordered by the Atlas Mountains and to the south the Niger river valley. It includes mountain chains like the Ahaggar and Tibesti ranges as well as volcanoes, rivers, salt flats, towns and cities and of course the rolling sand dunes that we were visiting. Stretching into Algeria, Chad, Egypt, Libya, Mali, Mauritania, Morocco, Niger, Western Sahara, Sudan and Tunisia the deserts climate ranges from the most arid lands in Libya to a more Mediterranean climate where we were. Cairo, Tripoli and Timbuktu can all be found within its confines. It is not devoid of vegetation either with some sparse grassland and some desert shrub areas to be found in the extreme north and south of the region and these are home to snakes, scorpions and rodents who all thrive in this environment. I won't list them all but there are at least forty types of rodent alone who live here and I haven't even mentioned the insects. There are of course many larger mammals as well and that brings me back to the camels we were here to ride. Preparations began before we even got near the camels as some locals excitedly greeted us and one of them attached himself to us. He spoke no English but gestured at us to follow him, which we did, and he led us to a huge and seemingly random pile of bits of old cloth. Our new friend took a step backwards from us, looked us up and down and then strode into the giant pile of cloth emerging after about half a minute with two robes which he held in outstretched arms for us to take. It was basically a very baggy t-shirt which we found stretched down to our ankles once we had put it on over our heads, carefully trying to maneuver our hands into the sleeves as we wrestled with the billowing fabric. The once possibly white garment was given its final adjustments by our host so it was hanging squarely from our shoulders and then he scooped up a pink sheet about the size of a hand towel which he threw over my head covering my face completely. He held the sheet in place with his hand next to my forehead and gripped and twisted the fabric that was hanging down across my face and in one effortless movement it was transformed into a head garment to shield me from the sun with a strip of the fabric stretching down across and protecting my neck. He repeated the process on Shaun which I watched carefully hoping to emulate the technique later (which I did and still can) and then with a big smile and another hand gesture we were led onwards. Around the corner of a nearby building, lying on the ground waiting for us were several dozen foul smelling, evil tempered camels. They are complete and utter bastards. Believe me when I tell you that as soon as one of these things sees you they develop a pathological hatred of you and will do everything in their power to do you harm. Our new-found friend again looked us up and down and then surveyed the choice of camels before him, his eyes flitting across all the options before coming to rest on a suitable steed. He took me by the arm and led me over to a large, irritable, spitting beast of a camel that was making a noise like some terrible demon from the seventh circle of hell and with a smile that to me looked a little less smiley than earlier he slapped the bare back of the creature indicating for me to jump on. I managed to get my leg high enough to swing over its rear hump and plopped into place with all the grace of a sack of potatoes which was a good job because the second it felt my backside come into contact with its back it stood up! If you have never seen this they get up onto their back legs first which suddenly leaves you sitting on a surface which is now at an angle of 45 degrees with nothing to hold onto. A steadying hand from our guide prevented me doing a forward role off the damn thing and face planting in the floor of the desert. Having witnessed me and having assessed the situations potential pitfalls Shaun was on his camel and up and ready to ride with the minimum of fuss which then gave us time to look around some of the rest of our group. There were about twenty of us in this group and we probably exchanged names with most of them but I've really no clue what they were now. There were two young Scottish men travelling together who we speculated may have been a couple, right up until we overheard them talking about the two young women who were friends from school and were doing some travelling in their gap year. Their conversation would have made a Lorry Driver blush and shan't be repeated here. These two couples were near to us at the back of the coach (we had got the back seat of course so we could stretch out) along with some honeymooners who made you feel nauseous when you were in their presence and an elderly couple who didn't seem to like each other very much. The rest of the group all crowded at the front of the coach and as we were quite happy with each other's company, reading our books, listening to music and staring out of the window we hadn't really interacted with them. The camel ride was however very much a group activity and we now had to wait while the rest of the group were dressed and taken over for camel selection and mounting. It was distracting in a there's nothing else to watch sort of way, at least it was until the elderly couple who didn't like each other arrived and the level of entertainment increased greatly. Entirely prepared and showing great confidence the wife stepped forward, steadied herself then raised her leg in a high arc to straddle the beast. The high arc wasn't high enough and she failed to get past the rear hump, stalled and slipped down with one leg either side of its arse. This was enough of a prompt for the camel to immediately stand up leaving the poor lady desperately holding on to the hump in front of her with legs left dangling. The animal's keepers and some brave locals rushed over and all cupped a handful of her backside which was beginning a gentle slide towards the ground under the irresistible influence of gravity. There was a good deal of shouting, pushing and shoving in a great melee of activity around her as they fought to drag her into the seating position and all the while the husband never moved a muscle. That's not quite true, he did crack a smile, the biggest smile I saw on him during the entire trip and their almost seemed to be an air of disappointment when the efforts of half a dozen by-standers finally got his wife atop the camel and ready to ride. With all the group finally mounted we were led out into the Sahara and into the great and seemingly never-ending expanse of sand dunes that lay before us. The term sand dunes doesn't quite seem to do them justice. It brings to mind the rolling dunes at Gibraltar point south of Skegness or possibly the little undulations to be found in Rhyl but the dunes that we were riding into stood 40 to 50 feet high and these were mere babies compared to their big brothers deeper in the interior which can stand up to well over 500 feet high. Astonishingly these massive things move. If you were to film the desert and then speed up the footage the dunes will behave much like the waves on the sea, flowing across the landscape driven by the winds. There are even people who study them, try to understand them, the forces behind them, the ecology of them and so forth and they have even found the time to divide them up into different categories rather than viewing them as I do as a giant pile of sand. There are Linear dunes, Crescentic, Dome, Parabolic, Reversing,

Star, Longitudinal dunes and these could all be coastal dunes or Nabkha dunes (inland) which makes them different apparently. There is a dune in China which stands at 1600 feet high and even more astonishingly to my mind one in France which stands some 1000 feet high. This does not square with my image of France which consists of Chateaux's, rustic farmhouses, vineyards, bicycles with onions draped over the handlebars and hyper-markets filled with cheap booze. Not a thousand-foot-tall pile of sand.

As we traced out a gentle circular route through the desert which would eventually return us to our start point we were not alone. The whole area was a hive of activity including loud and dirty 4x4's roaring around, kids sledging, micro-lights flying above and even a couple of men horse racing. The horses were finding it very hard going as there is an awful lot of horse per square inch of hoof and they were sinking into and kicking up large amounts of sand with every step. Unlike our camels of course which have very large and very soft feet which meant we were barely even leaving a visible foot print behind us. That coupled with their ability to store water as fat in the hump made them the ideal 'ship of the desert' and guaranteed them a role in this region that has lasted for millennia. Our ride was to last for about thirty minutes and before we knew it we were dismounting, being stripped of our robes and being given none too subtle gestures that a tip was very much expected. We faced another long journey now and dozing on the coach seemed a good way to pass the time. We would need the rest as we had to be up at three in the morning for a drive into the Salt Flats where we would watch the sun rise.

The climate here was not always so dry and thousands of years ago the whole area would have enjoyed torrential downpours of rain, high humidity, a lush canopy of vegetation stretching as far as the eye can see and the whole area was interspersed with many, many lakes. Very large lakes which remained in place as the climate shifted until eventually the drought and heat dried them out leaving the bed completely exposed. A flat bed devoid of features and carpeted with the Salt and other minerals left behind as the water evaporated. These are the Salt Flats, or Salt Pans of the Sahara. In the cool early hours of the morning our coach would take a single road out into this wilderness, driving for hours until we reached a point where nothing was visible in any direction except the never-ending flatness of the salt. From here we could experience day break with nothing getting in the way. Nothing that is except the honeymooning couple who were notable by their absence from the coach. A drowsy and slightly irritable group of people, including myself and Shaun were sat shivering on the, as yet, unheated coach. The engine was not running, the driver was stood outside smoking and spitting into the hotel flower-beds and our guide who had disappeared after conducting a head count and realising that two were missing had not been seen for a quarter of an hour. It was easy to detect a mood developing on the coach, an ugly mood that said if this honeymooning couple didn't have a damn good reason for being late, such as death, then there would definitely be some seriously dirty looks given. There was a possibility that people might even tut. After twenty minutes and just at the point where a lady at the front suggested we leave them behind with any consequences clearly being there own fault, they emerged from the hotel laughing and joking with the guide.

Boarding the coach they attempted a little bonhomie with us, their fellow passengers, explaining how they weren't morning people and only after the guide's banging on their door had woken half a dozen other guests did they finally stir from their slumber. 'Oh, what scallywags we are' they clearly thought to themselves, only slightly phased by the look of burning hatred from a coach full of seriously pissed off fellow passengers. We sat in silence for the next couple of hours, trying to wake up and wondering if it would be worth it. It was.

We eventually parked up at the side of the road whilst it was still dark but dawn was breaking and we were just about to head into twilight, that little slice of the day where the sky is light but the Sun has not yet popped up over the horizon. Shaun was stood still scanning the sky with a confused look on his face and when I asked what was wrong he replied,

"Where's the Sun?"

"It's not up yet."

"but its light?"

I didn't speak at this point but what I was thinking would have been written all over my face. He had never seen a sun rise before, or at least never noticed a sun rise before and didn't realise that it gets light before the Sun comes up. This from someone who knows the difference between the Financial Services Authority and the Financial Conduct Authority and who uses sentences like;

"CII compliance and regulatory focus are not sufficient in and of themselves but are a step to T.C.F. compliance and suitable customer outcomes."

For all I know that might actually mean something so its quite reassuring that he doesn't know it gets light before the Sun comes up! When he was little he also believed that power stations were 'cloud factories' where the clouds were manufactured and released from the big chimneys into the sky. I think that makes me love him a little bit more. We ambled about for a while looking for a good vantage point away from the coach and our fellow travelers and found a suitable spot off to one side. We stood and watched in silence as the top of the sun breached the horizon and began to rise into the morning sky. You can't look straight at the sun of course because it will make you blind so we watched it on the screen of our cameras, you can of course see the spectacular colours that surround it in these first few minutes as it rises into a clear morning sky. The Sun of course isn't rising, it remains exactly where it is and the rotation of the Earth moves the horizon creating the optical illusion that it's rising. It's very easy to see how people in the past with little or no scientific equipment and only their senses to guide them would have believed that the Earth was fixed in place and the Sun and all the other stars orbited around us. That said, it is now four centuries since Copernicus came up with the heliocentric model that places the Sun at the centre of our Solar System and we still use the terms 'sunrise' and 'sunset' even though they are so blatantly wrong. To my knowledge only the architect Buckminster Fuller proposed fixing this by using the terms 'sunsight' and 'sunclipse' instead but this never caught on. If you have never heard of him then please find the time to read up on Richard Buckminster Fuller or 'Bucky' as he was sometimes known. He was an American born in the late 19th century who became an architect, author, designer and inventor. By the age of 12 he had developed a new means of propulsion for a rowboat involving a submerged umbrella. He studied machine's and became proficient in the sheet metal trade and then developed a new method of production for house construction. He studied at Harvard, being expelled twice, once for lack of interest in his subject and the other time for spending all his money partying with a vaudeville troupe which I think is a fantastic reason to be expelled. He is perhaps most famous for the geodesic dome in his architectural work, a dome structure that could support its own weight with no practical limits and although he didn't invent the idea he did get the patent for it in the United States and popularised it. It is a design used in thousands of buildings all over the world from civil construction projects, military use such as radar stations and exhibition centres like the biosphere that was built in Montreal. His close association with the concept led to a group of scientists naming a carbon molecule after him (fullerenes) for their mathematical similarity to the dome's structure. He served as a radio operator and rescue boat commander in the U.S. Navy during World War I and as World President of Mensa in the 1970's and 80's. He referred to himself as the 'property of the universe' and declared himself and his work the 'property of all humanity' which seems pretty grand and at the same time reasonable when you look at his achievements. He was named Humanist of the Year 1969 and was a key participant at U.N. Habitat I which was the first U.N. forum on the sustainable development of human settlements. He coined the phrase 'spaceship earth' to try and make us look at ourselves differently, to realise that we rely on this planet of ours and its resources to sustain us in the vastness and blackness of space so we had better look after it. He wrote 30 books, received honours too numerous to list, appeared on film (search him on you tube), developed ideas ranging over topics from architecture to design, engineering, conservation, economics and much more and during the 1920's he even spent two years of his life experimenting with polyphasic sleep. This was inspired by the sleep pattern of cats and dogs which led him to sleep for just half an hour every six hours meaning that he had twenty two hours a day for thinking and making himself more productive. It was reported that he only stopped because it clashed so badly with the sleep cycle of all his associates. It's not all that practical if you're the only one doing it I guess. Throughout the 1960's and 1970's he was estimated to have spent only sixty days a year at home and the rest of the time was spent working and lecturing and he found himself frequently visiting multiple time zones in one journey. That led him to wear three watches, one with the time back home, one with the time where he was and one with the time where he was going to be next. He lived to the age of 87 when he died from a heart attack while visiting his comatose wife in hospital. She passed away just two days later. You could write a book with stories about him alone and the things he achieved but I had best leave that to someone else and get back to the salt flats.

As the sun rose the sky filled with colour and warmth. From the second the Sun's topmost part breached the horizon the warmth of its rays quickly dispersed the morning chill. Silence had descended over our group. In the silence and stillness of our companions my attention was drawn to the honeymoon couple who were just a few metres from me. The wife was down on one knee with her hands outstretched and cupped together. The husband was maneuvering himself and his camera around in order to capture a shot where his wife would be holding the rising Sun in her hands. A treasured memory for them to share. It makes you want to barf doesn't it. The Sun was now reaching a height where the colours on the horizon were fading but the temperature was now rapidly rising and it was time to move on to our next destination, Matmata and a nearby oasis. It was to be a long drive and we were grateful for the cooling breeze from the coach's air conditioning. We settled onto the back seat, leaning against opposite windows, facing each other with our feet up and reading our books as the coach sped along the desert road. After about half an hour we were disturbed by a loud bang which seemed to originate from directly beneath us. Instinctively we both looked up and out the rear window in time to see a long, thin piece of black rubber skittling down the road behind us.

"we must have hit it" I said thinking out loud,

We soon discovered we hadn't hit it. It wasn't some random piece of detritus lying in the road, it was in fact the drive belt for the air conditioning system which had come loose, creating the loud bang under our seat before falling out onto the road and being left behind. The coach became hotter, much hotter over the next half hour alerting the driver to the fact that something was wrong and causing him to pull over so he could inspect the Air-con unit which, he was now aware, was unresponsive. People were just beginning to fidget, armpits were becoming moist and sticky and clothing uncomfortable. We looked out the back window and saw the driver appear, lift up the rear hatch to gain access to the engine and after a minute or so he walked back and re-boarded the coach. We could all hear as he spoke to our guide,

"The drive belt's gone!"

I swear to god he turned and looked straight at me and Shaun on the back seats and followed up with,

"I can't believe no one heard it come off!"

We both did our best to look innocent as several dozen heads turned to give us an accusing look. Alright, that might not have happened but it certainly felt like it and in fairness to us how the hell were we supposed to know? With no other option the driver resumed his seat and we continued with our now very hot and sweaty coach journey. After what seemed like a lifetime we arrived in Matmata.

This little town is famous for its troglodyte communities or cave dwellers to use the vernacular. The entire town has been built by digging down into the ground rather than building up. All the rooms of the houses are in the cool underground and even the courtyards are sunk below ground level so on the surface from a distance you wouldn't even realise that anything was here. It is a unique location and attracted the interest of Hollywood who filmed scenes for the Star Wars films here including, most famously, Luke Skywalker's desert homestead which in reality is the Hotel Sidi Driss and was originally a Berber home. Skywalker's home was a desert planet so the film crew must have been thrilled on their arrival when the area suffered one of its worst rainstorms for fifty years! There is a simple repeating pattern used for these habitations which begins with a shaft dug vertically down to a depth of two stories, the bottom of which will be the family's courtyard, a staircase will circle the outside of this with cave's dug into the surrounding rock. We saw some cave entrances left open and some covered with cloth but most had bright blue wooden doors in place which would open on to the living quarters. Such is the fame and popularity of this place the coaches arrive all day long with a never-ending stream of tourists crowding around and peering down into these people homes. In response, whatever their original means of earning a living were have been abandoned in favour of selling tours of their homes and souvenirs, some hand crafted, some mass produced to their now captive audience. If you are so inclined you can even pay to spend the night in one of the caves to experience how these people live. We were not so inclined and were happy to take photos and then head back to a comfy hotel and our balcony with a nice view and possibly a bottle of wine. These rooms have no windows, no view, no matter how comfortable they are it's not my idea of a holiday. The kitchen areas had a mixture of storage from cubby holes and shelves calved directly into the rock to ceramic food pots some of which are several feet high which are passed down as family heir looms. Earlier on I said that as you looked at this place you wouldn't realise there was a settlement here. That actually isn't true anymore as during the 1960's there was a terrible storm in Tunisia and this area received over 20 days of near continuous rainfall deluging these dwellings and rendering them uninhabitable. In response the government sent help to the region. They thought they were going to help the nomadic peoples of the area with flood relief and were apparently surprised to find a permanent underground town of several thousand people who were now homeless. In that high handed, big brother knows best way of all governments everywhere an above ground settlement was created for the population to move into which some people did. Many however refused viewing it as a direct assault on their customs, history and way of life and instead repaired their underground dwellings or built new ones. They then went back to living their traditional lifestyle. Traditional apart from the film crews, Star Wars props and streams of tourists which would appear over the next two decades of course. The props that were to be found included the skeleton of a creature called a Greater Krayt Dragon which inhabited this fictional planet of Tatooine. After filming had finished this skeleton was left in the desert and when the crews returned in 2002 for Star Wars II - Attack of the Clones they visited the area and discovered that the prop was still there and fully intact.

It's a bit unfair of me to suggest that their traditions were no more, there was plenty of evidence of traditions here that were still a normal, everyday part of their life. We saw women using stones to grind down wheat that was used to make Tabouna, a type of bread baked in a terracotta oven and which is still widely produced. The inside of the caves are still painted with lime which will help to capture light from the bright desert outside, bouncing it around and lifting the gloom, and above many of the doorways are still symbols of the fish and of the hand. The fish is seen as a good luck charm and the hand, or more accurately it's fingers are seen to represent the five pillars of Islam. The power of these symbols together represents their faith and they believe will protect their homes. The five pillars are;

Shahadah; Reciting the profession of faith.

Salat: Performing ritual prayers five times a day.

Zakat: Giving to charity for the poor and needy.

Sawm: Fasting during the month of Ramadan.

Hajj: pilgrimage to Mecca.

Their faith is central to their life rather than just being fitted in around it when it's convenient. With that last nugget of information explained to us by a local for a very reasonable donation we were done and whisked away in a fleet of waiting Landrover's to see a nearby oasis. The journey felt long as we bumped around on dirt tracks for what seemed like an age but which eventually led us to a parking area from where we had to proceed on foot up a steep incline. This turned into a two-foot-wide path across a cliff face with an arsehole-twitching sheer drop to one side. We climbed and sweated and climbed some more until we reached the summit and looked down into a valley of lush greenery, framed on all sides by the endless baron rock of the desert. This tiny valley tucked away had a natural spring which provided enough water to support a miniature eco-system of palm trees, grasses, vegetation and flowers and that was home to a community of about a dozen people. Small shacks populated the slopes of the valley with a communal living area straddling the central stream. It seemed quiet and undisturbed except for a noise that I couldn't quite identify that seemed to hang over us. We were greeted by one of the locals as though we were old friends and asked if we required refreshment after our arduous climb. We certainly did and accepting his offer stepped into a nearby hut expecting some sort of fruit juice, perhaps tea or coffee but certainly not the rows of refrigerators packed with Coca Cola and various other fizzy treats. The unidentified noise was a petrol generator chugging away at the back of this shack to power the fridges. Was this worth it? Dragging a generator and fridges up here, not to mention the cost and hassle of getting the petrol topped up and then the supplies of pop that would need to be brought in. They then charged me

£5 for a 500ml bottle of coke and I realised that it was definitely worth it.

An oasis like the one we were visiting is simply an isolated area of vegetation in a desert. It could be around a spring as this one was with its gently babbling stream which disappeared back into the desert after a few hundred metres but it may also be a small pond or even a lake. It provides a sanctuary for animals and humans if its big enough. It may result from an underground river being forced to the surface or by rainfall from the occasional thunderstorm being trapped by a substrata of impermeable rocks. Whatever the cause as soon as there is a source of water on the surface it will be a focal point for migrating birds who will stop off there to refresh themselves and depositing seeds from their droppings into the surrounding area. These seeds will then grow into the trees, shrubs and flowers which in turn can support more complex life. Excluding the Nile Valley there are a couple of million people living within the Sahara including nomadic tribes as well as permanent settlements and they and the trade they generate rely entirely on the locations of these oasis. The trade routes must follow the availability of water and so these areas became of vital strategic importance to the people and the Empires that wished to control the region. Control an Oasis and you control the trade putting you in a very powerful position. Not only was the water vital to the trade routes but the vegetation, particularly the dates were an important part of the local economy on their own. Many battles were fought for their control and a short distance over the border in Algeria the French Armee d'Afrique suffered one of its most humiliating defeats at one such place. It is 1849 and the French Empire includes the nation of

Algeria. Not unreasonably the people of Algeria are not happy at being subjugated in this way and an uprising has taken place against French rule in the south of the country. The spark was taxation on the date trees that were so vital to the livelihoods of the locals. The authorities were deeply concerned that this uprising may spread north into the Mediterranean coastal areas and so they responded as Empires do with the deployment of a big stick to beat the rebels down. The rebellion was led by a man named Bouzian who was once Caid of Zaatcha, an oasis in the deep south of the country. A number of successful battles, particularly the defeat of the Ouled-Sahnoun tribe through sheer intimidation, including the chopping down of date trees which were there main source of income, buoyed the French forces led by Jean-Luc Carbuccia whose self-confidence and arrogance was about to lead them into disaster. The not untypical belief amongst Empire types that they were morally and physically superior to the natives led him into over-confidence, underestimating his enemies in the Zaatcha oasis whom he had been tasked to sort out. He regarded them as nothing more than a bunch of gardeners who would have no stomach for a fight. Unconcerned by the fact that he had only lightly armed infantrymen and little by way of cavalry he decided to proceed directly on the rebel oasis and to take down Bouzian without delay. He marched his soldiers through the scorching Sahara in temperatures north of 130 degrees Fahrenheit, temperatures that made it an effort to even breathe and arrived at the strong-hold with his men completely knackered. The strong-hold from his vantage point appeared deceptively tranquil and unassuming. Nothing more than a blanket of deep green date palms surrounded by the sandy desert. It can hardly have seemed a serious military obstacle to these highly experienced military men and Carbuccia didn't bother to perform any reconnaissance. When his men were unexpectedly attacked by the rebels who came streaming out of the trees instead of just holding their ground (as Carbuccia claims he ordered) his men still weary and un-rested ran at the enemy. They discovered that this was not such a tranquil place and on entering the tree cover discovered heavily fortified walls from which a great many of their number were shot and killed leading to a retreat. Worrying that this show of weakness would embolden the enemy the French troops were divided into two columns and after a brief speech to motivate them for the battle they descended on their target. Almost immediately the pleasant looking landscape became a quagmire of tangled roots, mud walls, stagnant moats and enemy fortifications. Disorientated and confused they wandered straight into the zone of fire that lay before one of the most fortified parts of the area where they were cut down with little resistance. After a chaotic retreat Carbuccia spent three days considering the situation before deciding to give up and march back north. The Arabs saw him off with some rousing singing. His claim to the French War Minister that although he had not been successful he had definitely terrified the Arabs was not well received and the whole episode was never forgotten by his fellow officers or indeed history.

We had by this point finished our drinks, wandered around aimlessly pausing at the stream to confirm that yes, it is water, and were now beginning the journey back down to our coach. We would stop for some early afternoon refreshments before beginning the long drive back to our hotel in Port el Kantaoui. The day was getting steadily hotter but our driver had shown some initiative and had somehow found a replacement belt out here in the middle of nowhere and at least we were now kept cool as we whiled away the time till dinner. The hotel where dinner was to be served was amazing especially as when we pulled up and parked at a desolate spot on top of a hill we couldn't even see it. All that was visible was a stone staircase carved into the rock floor curving away in front of us. Following it down we were presented with a set of automatic doors with tinted glass in a sheer rock face. These slid open to reveal a large marble hall carved into the mountain. Our hotel was carved into the ground Matmata style. The dining area was large with one entire wall a floor to ceiling window flush with the cliff outside offering panoramic views of the surrounding hills. It was a sparse meal to be honest, buffet style with rice and a selection of meats all of which contained a lot of bones and all tasting of olive oil and little else. When we had finished we had the chance to wander for a few minutes and thought we would have a look around. We found a small terrace area outside with a pool and some sun-loungers and wandering past that and deeper into the complex we found the guest rooms. This place was a hole, literally. One of the biggest holes I have ever seen in fact. Probably 40 metres long on each side they had dug straight down into the rock from ground level and then dug into the sides of this monstrous pit to create the rooms. I can't attest to how comfortable it was but as unusual hotels go this was right up there with the best of them. Unfortunately we ran out of time at this point and began the long drive back to our hotel where as good fortune would have it a bottle of wine was waiting to be drunk on our balcony. A very acceptable ending to the day and to our holiday I'm afraid and so it's time to leave Tunisia and move on to our next destination, Morocco.

MOROCCO

Morocco was another last minute and hastily organised package holiday which found us heading to the seaside town of Agadir. Officially known as the Kingdom of Morocco it is located in the Maghreb region of north-west Africa, its interior dominated by rugged mountains, large areas of desert and a long coastline with both the Atlantic Ocean and the Mediterranean Sea. Unusually, and unlike many of its neighbours they have managed to maintain their independence for most of the time since its foundation in 789 by Idris I and has been ruled by a series of dynasties ever since. Unusually, they were one of a handful of countries who petitioned to be admitted to the British Empire voluntarily although the British declined to accept them. They are the only north African country who avoided occupation by the Ottoman Empire and their independence remained intact all the way up to 1912 when they finally succumbed to European Imperialism, in this case the French and Spanish, from whom they won their independence again in 1956 after just over four decades. France controlled the Lion's share of the country but the Spanish had protectorates agreed by treaty in a small northern strip including the Strait of Gibraltar (opposite British Gibraltar on the tip of southern Spain) and a strip in the south around Cape Juby. The Spanish areas of control were gifted to them as a result of the Entente Cordial between Britain and France in 1904 which was designed to carve up the world into spheres of interest thus removing the need for them to fight any more wars with each other and enabling them to concentrate on fighting wars with everybody else. The

Spanish had declined the areas north of the Sebu River and South of the Sous River in Morocco just four years earlier when offered to them by the French for fear of upsetting the British so of course once the British had agreed to it they were more than happy to add these places to their zone of influence. At no point did anybody speak to the Moroccans about what they might consider to be in their best interests. As of 1956 when independence was gained from France, Spain did cede control of some of their areas back to the new Kingdom but attempted to hold on to control in a few strategically important areas which resulted in a war, a war that Spain ultimately lost but which did leave them with control of Ceuta and Melilla, areas that even today they view as an inseparable part of their country. Ceuta has been described as being to Spain what Gibraltar is to the British. These are areas that Morocco still considers to be an integral part of its own land and regards as being under enemy occupation and as recently as 2002 a diplomatic crisis broke out over control of a deserted island less than 200 metres from the Moroccan coast which they call Toura and which the Spanish call Perejil. A crisis that necessitated the involvement of the United States no less who brokered a peace deal returning the island to the status quo under which it remains deserted. As always it seems the history of Imperialism has left one gigantic simmering mess of resentment, disagreement and grudge holding.

This part of Africa is one of the few places in the world where British military adventurism and occupation never really got going and during the early part of the seventeenth century our relations with the Moroccan people were in fact rather warm and cordial. The Sultan of

Morocco, Ahmad al-Mansur and Queen Elizabeth I got on rather well together and found they had much in common, most especially their mutual hatred and distrust of the Spanish and their King, Philip II. There was plenty of trade and the odd discussion about launching joint attacks on Spanish interests in the area and we even engaged in some joint operations against Pirates which all sounds rather splendid. Things did sour a little for a few years in the latter part of the century when we ended up in control of the port of Tangiers in the north of the country. We didn't take it by force but were given it by the Portuguese as a wedding gift when Charles II married Catherine of Braganza which seems a little excessive and certainly wouldn't feature on the average wedding list, not even at John Lewis. After less than thirty years we chose to walk away as the value of our naval base there was felt to be less than the damage caused to our relationship with the Kingdom so in a magnanimous gesture we blew up all the buildings that might have been of any use to them and walked away! There was, to my knowledge, only one occasion since when British forces acted in anger in Morocco and that was during the Second World War. The country had found itself under occupation by the Nazi's and in 1942 the American's launched Operation Torch which consisted of large amphibious landings along the coastline and which was designed to liberate both Morocco and Algeria from their occupation. While it was almost entirely an American led and staffed operation the British Escort Carrier H.M.S. Archer did take part and arrived in Casablanca bringing troops and equipment to help the fight.

As already mentioned we were staying in Agadir which is the country's largest seaside resort and like many other places we have stayed it is purpose built for it. Unlike some of the other places the opportunity for redevelopment was afforded by a massive earthquake in 1960 which utterly destroyed the area and required a complete reconstruction from scratch, this time under strict anti-quake standards. It sits on the Atlantic coast some 500 kilometres south of Casablanca and close to where the Sous river joins the sea and has found favour with northern Europeans thanks to an abundance of cheap flights and an all year-round moderate climate. The only surviving part of the old town is an almost destroyed Casbah, an ancient walled fortress where about the only original feature still to be seen is an inscription over the front door which reads 'Fear God and Honour the King' an inscription which still seems pretty apt for the country today. The inscription is in Dutch as well as Arabic and attests to the Dutch excursion into the region with the establishment of trading posts and support for the rebuilding of the community after it was destroyed in a large earthquake in 1731.

Our journey was uneventful as was our arrival at the hotel, a perfectly charming oasis of tranquillity which was close to the beach and surrounded on all sides by a thoroughly modern and buzzing town. Before travelling it is my preference to undertake an internet search of the hotels we are visiting just to get an idea of what to expect. Typing in the name of our hotel and its location I was a little bemused to find the first search result was; 'mysterious mother and child deaths still unexplained'. This is not what I was expecting! Regardless of what happened to that unfortunate family we found on our arrival that there was nothing to fear. High walls surrounded the hotel on all sides and on entering the main gate we found ourselves in something more like a village than a hotel. There were extensive gardens with multiple swimming pools, restaurants and bars all interspersed with small blocks of hotel rooms no more than 3 stories high with only 12 rooms in each block and a central courtyard which was shaded and cool with an impressive array of marble tiles around it. Access was through this central courtyard and up an internal staircase that led to the rooms. This design allowed the outside to be available for a large balcony area, every one of which had a pleasant view over the landscaped grounds. The whole complex was built on a slope and one of the first things mentioned in the brochure and in bold print no less was that this place was unsuitable for people of limited mobility due to the aforementioned slope, sets of steps and lack of lifts in any of the small blocks of rooms. It should therefore come as no surprise that when we went down to visit the Travel Rep we found ourselves waiting behind two British pensioners who were bitterly complaining about how unsuitable the hotel was for people of their limited mobility and demanding to know what the Rep proposed to do about it. She proved to be a remarkably patient lady who listened with great care to the customers concerns, customers who in my humble opinion were more deserving of a slap than the concern and understanding they were in fact receiving. She sorted them a replacement room on the ground floor of one of the buildings next to a swimming pool, bar and one of the many restaurants and after well over half an hour these two grey haired morons finally shuffled off still mumbling to themselves about how ridiculous it was. Turning her attention to us with repeated apologies for the wait we were ushered into some comfy seats opposite her and after a brief introduction she began the hard sell on some exciting excursions to fill our week. Agadir is not badly situated for touring at least parts of the country. We were clearly too far from Tangiers or Casablanca in the north as we were only here for a week and they would have involved substantial journeys but we were within easy reach of the Atlas mountains to the north, the old towns of Tiznit and Tafraout in the anti-atlas mountains to the south and Marrakech to the East. She kindly sorted out the appropriate days, made the relevant booking, issued us with our receipts and tickets for our tours and bid us goodbye. She could now deal with the family waiting behind us who's impatience was becoming more pronounced especially when they thought we had finished and then we asked about booking another trip. We had a couple of days before our first organised trip which gave us time to do a little exploring of Agadir itself which is one of the largest urban centres in Morocco, as well it should be considering that it is made up of no fewer than four separate towns which have all merged together. The former town of Agadir city which has been rebuilt, the towns of Ben Sergao and Tikiwine and the smaller community of Anza. The country has a large foreign debt and suffers from high levels of unemployment with one of the few strong growth and employment areas being tourism. The success of the tourist trade here and the jobs it has brought has resulted in a large influx of people from rural areas seeking work, according to one local I was chatting with the number of houses is growing by only half the rate needed to keep up with the growing demand which is causing a lot of problems. The seafront and beach here are everything you could wish them to be. Sitting in a gently arcing bay there is a wide sandy beach, multiple opportunities for refreshment, gently swaying palm trees and a mountainous headland to the north with the three words Allah, Nation and King which at night are illuminated by floodlights and are visible from miles along the coast. Having taken a short stroll along the front and having found a supermarket where we could buy soft drinks and wine to be smuggled back into our room thus avoiding the extortionate bar charges and then opted for a lazy afternoon by one of the pools. Typically there were about 73 guests for every available sun-lounger but we persevered and eventually settled down for a chilled afternoon. I have always preferred a swimming pool to the sea due to a deep concern about what might be lurking just below the surface. This is possibly due to my parents letting me watch Jaws when I was only 8 years old and reinforced by a holiday to Wales a year later where I found myself unexpectedly surrounded by half of the world's jelly fish. As an adult my fear was reinforced when I was swimming off a secluded beach in Venezuela and a snake of at least six feet in length appeared just a few metres from me and began swimming in my direction. Now Michael Phelps may officially be the fastest swimmer in the world but that afternoon if I didn't beat him I at least ran him a pretty close second! Our tour guide's assertion that;

"This sort of thing almost never happens!" was not totally reassuring. Even if some creature doesn't bite, stab or poison you a rogue rip-tide might grab you at any moment and drag you off to a watery grave. No, a swimming pool is definitely the place for me as it's just safer. During one particularly dull morning at home, lying in bed with only the Google App on my smart-phone for company I found myself reading a report by the Royal Society for the Prevention of Accidents who were looking into the safety of pools, baths and ponds and who found that in the U.K. in 2005 twelve times as many people died in the bath as in a swimming pool which is reassuring about the pool but a little alarming about the bath. Mind you, if you think we have it bad in the U.K. just be grateful that you don't live in Japan where they have the most dangerous baths in the world. In 2004 3,429 people were reported to have died in the bath which even adjusting for population is 68 times higher than the risk back home. I have given some thought to this (I get bored at work sometimes) and can offer no sensible explanation as to what could possibly make taking a bath such a lethal pass time. That said, safe is a relative term and you do need to exercise some caution when using a swimming pool abroad (Standby for a Public Service Announcement). Most pools at home are covered by strict safety laws that require the presence of Lifeguards and safety equipment as well as regular and specified testing for water cleanliness and de-contamination processes. In many place we Brits travel to on holiday no such rules exist and the poolside can become a much more dangerous place especially for unsupervised children who's ability to get into trouble in a matter of seconds is even greater than mine. Even if you manage not to drown a badly maintained pool is a breeding ground for germs that offer an exciting array of ways to get ill during your holiday. Here are just a few examples:

Shigellosis or bacillary dysentery is an easily transferable disease that causes fever, nausea, vomiting, cramps and diarrhea and will cause a mucus filled bloody stool which is not something you would want to write home about.

E.Coli is a major cause of infections in hospitals and can also be present in a poorly maintained pool. Your stool won't just contain blood it will be ALL blood as your intestinal tract suffers hemorrhagic colitis. If left untreated, or even if it is treated, it may lead to kidney failure.

Leptospirosis which is contracted from the urine of wild animals (all it takes is one rat in the pool) causes fever, chills, jaundice, rashes and blood haemorrhaging into your skin which would be more colourful than a tan but even less healthy.

Hepatitis A is a Virus that attacks the liver and won't respond to antibiotics. This is spread by the fecal-oral route which means if someone in the pool hasn't wiped their bum properly then little bits of their poo break off and float around until you stick your head under the water and it goes in your mouth.

Cryptosporidiosis is a parasitic infection that affects not only humans but over 40 other species including birds, fish, dogs, cats and cattle. You will get to experience fever, vomiting and anorexia and the infectious spores from it are resistant to the chemical disinfectants that are used to clean the water.

Norwalk Virus is most famous for spreading out of control on Cruise Ships and bringing misery to thousands. Also known as Epidemic Viral Gastroenteritis, Winter vomiting disease, Norwalk agent disease and many other names this one can be spread by the fecal-oral route as well as human to human contact and airborne transmission so this is one to share with friends and family.

Pseudomonas which causes ear and skin infections is one that loves a heated pool, not only does the warmth encourage the growth of the bacteria but it also breaks down the chemicals that are used to clean the pools and makes them less effective.

There are a few that are even more revolting such as Shistosomiasis which you can catch from water where any snails have been around. Cercariae which the snail releases can penetrate human skin and enter your bloodstream where they make their way to the blood vessels in your lungs. From here they migrate to the veins in your abdominal cavity and your liver. Symptoms will include diarrhoea, abdominal pain and an enlarged liver which may possibly lead to reduced liver function and colorectal cancer.

And the last one on my list for today is Drancunculiasis which is also known as Guinea worm disease. This is an infection in the subcutaneous tissue under your skin with a large nematode worm. This one will give you burning and itching skin, fever, nausea, vomiting and diarrhoea and most excitingly when the worm is ready to reproduce a large blister will form which when submerged in water will burst expelling all its larvae ready to start the cycle again.

This list is not exhaustive and there are many other disgusting infections you could catch but these things are of course very rare and it is most unlikely that you would contract anything. Saying that, the Centre for Disease Control in the United States undertook a study between 2000 and 2014 which looked at 27,219 cases of illnesses resulting from pathogens or chemicals and found that fully one third of these could be traced back to hotel swimming pools! Still, I think the main lesson to take away from this is that searching for things on the internet can be a really bad idea. A friend once wondered why the body's response to the cold is to make you shiver and so she searched 'why do I shiver?' According to the internet she probably had mercury poisoning. From all this we can safely conclude that on a hot day you should slap on some waterproof sun-cream and jump in for a cooling dip. You probably won't regret it.

Our first trip of the holiday saw us heading just over sixty miles south on a two-hour coach trip, or it would have been two hours were it not for two things. Firstly, as the coach pulled up and the driver stepped out to inspect our tickets we realised that we were the first to be collected and would therefore spend the next three quarters of an hour driving around the hotels of Agadir picking up the other guests. Secondly, we took an unexpected and un-requested toilet break half-way through the journey which itself lasted nearly half an hour. As we had only been driving for an hour and because we were all adults none of us required the use of the facilities. I personally had done my business before leaving the hotel and had very carefully ensured that a single sheet of toilet paper remained on the roll when I finished so that I wouldn't have to replace it. Job well done. As we had some free time to kill most of us purchased some coffee and snacks from the adjacent cafe. If I was feeling cynical I might suggest some sort of familial relationship between the driver and the owner of the service station could well have been behind our unscheduled stop. One or two members of the group lit up some foul smelling local cigarettes while they sipped their tar like coffee and gazed out over an entirely unprepossessing landscape. Arabic coffee is unlike any coffee that you are likely to have been served in Europe (apart from some trendy coffee shops, probably owned by a hipster with a man-bun and a tattoo) and it is all too easy to lump all the coffees served in

Arabic countries into one general heading but in fact there is a huge amount of variation in taste depending on how the beans are roasted and which flavourings are added. Many of the variations are regional with Turkish coffee being sweeter than most others, Jordanian coffee being lighter and intimately bound up with hospitality rather than as an every day drink and Moroccan coffee being somewhat more bitter and providing an excuse for the gathering of keen minds for intellectual discussions. Its role and taste vary and the above descriptions are a grotesque generalisation but hopefully you get the idea. They do all have a number of things in common though including their preparation on a stove in a purpose made pot called a dallah and then being served in a rather small (think espresso sized) cup called a finjaan. They all contain the Arabic coffee beans, water and usually cardamom and it will likely have the consistency of the melted tar on a British motorway on a hot day in June. Aside from the differences in the way the beans are roasted the flavour can be changed by the addition of cloves, rose water, saffron, ginger, orange blossom or cinnamon amongst other things, but rarely sugar as it is expected to be a bitter tasting drink. This is why you will often find yourself offered something sweet, like dates for example, to eat as you consume it. Oh, and you never ever add any milk except maybe a splash of evaporated milk to lighten the colour. It is impolite to refuse an offer of coffee from any of the locals, including from the owners of the souvenir shops that you might visit. We have found ourselves offered coffee in shops across a number of Arab countries and I can testify that they were always offered with nothing but hospitality in mind and no expectation of it securing a purchase from their establishment. Just be warned though, they will keep offering you a top up every time you get close to the bottom of your cup but the expectation is that you will decline any more after your third cup as to do otherwise would be seen as at least impolite if not downright greedy. Our unscheduled break was clearly drawing to a close and the fact that every passenger was sat back on the coach may have been a hint to our driver and guide that the time had come to drink up and crack on with the excursion. After a smooth ride along what was clearly a new road punctuated by occasional signs stating that 'This road project was financed with the aid of the European Union' (I can suggest several roads in Derbyshire equally deserving of some support) we finally arrived at our first proper destination of the day, Tiznit.

Tiznit is a small town of around fifty thousand people located in the Berber regions in the south of the country. The Berbers, a name derived from the Greek for barbarians, are native to North Africa and there are some 40 million of them residing mostly in Morocco and Algeria but with a smattering in Tunisia, Libya, Mali and Niger. In spite of attempts by the Romans, Arabs and various European powers to invade them they always successfully resisted and have preserved their society for somewhere near 4000 years until they were absorbed into the mix that is modern Morocco. Their rebelliousness in the Souss region was the reason that Tiznit was founded in the first place as in 1881 Sultan Moulay Hassan settled in the area in order to exert control over the dissident tribes and consolidate his power. It is a strategic location standing between the Sahara and the Atlantic coast and the Anti-Atlas mountains and the Tafraoute region. More than a century later as you visit you can enjoy places such as the Khalifa Palace, El Mechouar Place and the Grand

Mosque as well as the walled marketplace, the old Medina, which is enclosed by high walls on all sides and accessible via five gates known as Bab Aglou, Bag el Khemis, Bab Targa, Bab el Maader and Bab Oulad Jerrar. These are all impressive but you will probably find that you are drawn to the medina first to view the the finest jewellery and silver work in all the country and possibly the continent. The reputation for quality and workmanship in this area is known far and wide. You will find as you browse a selection of bracelets, necklaces, daggers, sabres, rifles, stones, enamels and pendants, all marked out by high quality and a reasonable and open to negotiation price. The silver work in particular was drawn from a strong Jewish tradition in the area with a population of nearly a third of a million residing here until the founding of Israel in 1948 after which the number has dwindled to just a few thousand. From 1940-1944 the country was controlled by the French who at that time were ruled by the Vichy government who collaborated with Nazi Germany and history has clearly recorded what they did to the Jews. The fact that there were still nearly a third of a million Jews in Morocco at the end of the war is a testament to King Mohamed V (The Sultan) amongst others. He was clearly constrained in how much he could achieve as he was only in place under the agreement of the French authorities and as a result some restrictions were placed on the Jewish people with some deported to work camps in the Sahara. In fact it was no worse for them than for Moroccan citizens who were also viewed as lesser citizens in their own country and found themselves subject to the same inhumane treatments. The Sultan did make a stand though. When a demand was received by his government from the Vichy/Nazi regime demanding a list be compiled of all the Jews resident in Morocco the response was simple;

"We have no Jews in Morocco, only Moroccan citizens"

His public stand extended to public events such as the annual Throne day where a number of senior Vichy officials were in earshot when the Sultan publicly welcomed Jewish community leaders and spoke in a voice loud enough for the French to hear saying,

"I must inform you that, just as in the past, the Israelites will remain under my protection. I refuse to make any distinction between my subjects."

A census was forced through and conducted but as soon as the Anglo-American invasion liberated the country all of the information gathered was immediately destroyed for the protection of the Jewish people. That is one rare spot of an almost happy ending for Jewish people since the Roman Conquest of Judaea and dispersal of their population some 2 millennia ago. For those that found their way to Morocco they were accepted, by and large, and were at home here until the 11th century when invading Muslims massacred thousands of their number and then forced those who survived to convert to Islam or be forced into exile. Some level of toleration was found over the next few centuries but tragedy never seemed very far away. For example in the town of Fez in 1465 many Jews were appointed to high positions in the town and this resulted in a revolt in which the entire Jewish community was massacred or exiled. Only three decades later Fez became a place of refuge from the murderous excess of Catholicism in Spain which led to violent outrages being perpetrated against the Jewish population there and leading to the Edict of the Expulsion of the

Jews by King Ferdinand and Queen Isabella. In 1492 they were driven from their homes and out of Spain with many now fleeing back to North Africa and Morocco for sanctuary. Some of those who fled Spain were the very same people who just a few years before had fled Morocco and who now found themselves acting as go-betweens for their people and the Berber tribes they found themselves living with again. One group eventually came to settle in Tiznit where a fortuitous set of circumstances has led to a reputation for silverwork that we see today.

Silver was in abundance in the region with a history of mining stretching back to the 1st century and so a Berber tradition of using silver was well established. The rising price of gold saw it supplanting silver in most places across the world but the Islamic tradition that had spread through this region had insulated the area from this change as certain texts of the Quran forbid the wearing of gold. Lastly the traditional crafts on which they had historically relied had come under fierce competition at a time of rising global trade, but when it came to the filigree work of their craftsmen they were more than a match for anyone. The Jews may be mostly gone from here now but their easily recognisable techniques are still in evidence. Not surprisingly jewellery occupies a prominent place in peoples every day lives and can serve several different purposes. The wearing of it may just be an adornment for fashion purposes but it may also be used as an indicator of social status or as a demonstration of wealth (just like back home I guess). There are also some more practical aspects with my favourite example being the jewellery given to a bride on her wedding day for whom these gifts represent her means of independence should her husband pass away and leave her as a widow. The rest of his wealth may well pass directly to any children rather than to the wife so the value of her wedding day adornments will be very important and may well include rings, bracelets, necklaces, earrings and topped off with headdresses imbedded with coins and possibly a cockerel in the design somewhere to help with her fertility. Although this tradition continues it is mostly costume jewellery that has been hired for the day as most of the family heirlooms were sold off long ago to deal with periods of hardship but I think it's still an interesting part of local history that is worth half a day of anyone's time. As is traditional on any organised excursion we were to finish off at a museum, or shop as it may be more accurately described where after a short presentation the selling began. As neither of us has any interest in demonstrating our social status or preparing for being a widow we excused ourselves from the melee and headed off outside. The history here may be engaging but the architecture certainly wasn't, at least not where we were so we passed the time with an ice-cold coke at a small café just up the road from where the coach would pick us up and whisk us away to our next stop, Tafraoute.

Tafraoute is a couple of hours drive by coach from Tiznit and the journey takes you some 70 miles inland away from the Atlantic coast. The scenery on this journey alone is enough to make it worthwhile as you head through the farm and scrub land of the anti-Atlas mountains. You pass by many fields of produce that are likely as not destined for the super-markets of western Europe and in the more open areas there is a good chance that you will see shepherds with their flocks of goats roaming the countryside looking for a good source of food. The grasses that grow naturally here are low in nutritional value so there is a chance that you will see the nimble goats climbing trees in search of Argan nuts. It is an unwritten law that the coach will stop and everyone will take a photo of this before continuing with the journey. Part of the drive will find you on a rapidly narrowing track which snakes wildly in different directions with boulders the size of a bus looming over you one moment and then sheer drops away from the road the next, sheer drops which would lead to certain death if the driver's concentration were to waver for just a moment. It is worth the risk though for on arrival you will find yourself presented with a perfect little town with low pink buildings, but not too many, populating a small shallow bowl flanked by rocky outcrops. A small cluster of minarets punctuate the skyline but are dwarfed by mighty granite cliffs climbing away from you in the middle distance. From the road into the town the Lion's head is visible, a gigantic granite peak belonging to the Anti-Atlas range and which is so-called because of the striking resemblance it has to a Lion's head. This is particularly stunning when it is hit by the late afternoon sun and it is well worth making the effort to be there at that time for that alone. It is no surprise given this location that we spotted a number of climbers in the town during our stay who were wanting to conquer these peaks. There are also groups of climbers who like bouldering, something which I had never heard of until this point which involves dozens of individual climbs in one day on all the granite boulders (or eggs as they're known) rather than one big climb up to the top of a mountain or cliff face. The predominate religion here as you may have guessed from the minarets is Islam and while the people are not as devout as some other parts of the world we were given some guidance on our behaviour so as not to cause offence, particularly in regard to the older inhabitants. Shorts for men and short skirts or dresses for women were inappropriate as your knees should be covered and no sleeveless t-shirts as your shoulders should also not be visible. The people here don't drink, which is like most of the rest of the country, but you will find it difficult to purchase alcohol here unlike most of the rest of the country which happily manufactures wines and beers for tourists to consume. They may not imbibe alcohol themselves but they take no offence at tourists having a tipple. As a general rule it is also a good idea not to take a photo of anyone unless you have asked their permission first and on that topic although it isn't for religious reasons you should not attempt to take any photos of any government buildings, soldiers or police if you see them. At best you will be made to delete the photos from your camera, at worst you could have your camera confiscated and you could find yourself under arrest. The attraction of this place had no particular focal point or at least it didn't for me, it was the town as a whole, its location, the little shops and the friendly people that combined to make this a place worth visiting. Most of the locals speak Berber or Arabic with a few understanding French and only a handful speaking English. As it happens those who speak English are the ones who are keenest on selling you something and they seem to have an ability to spot a Brit from about three hundred metres away. Paintings, ornaments, jewellery, chess boards, lamps, carpets, fabrics, spices, fruits, hats, nuts and all other manner of goods were displayed for our perusal with friendly but not overly pushy vendors vying for our business. Standing out from the crowd, and something we had been told about by our guide, were the shops that sold ordinary objects that have been re-purposed and which may be of practical use to the locals or as an interesting piece of tat for a tourist to take back home. Glass jars turned into lamps, old plastic carrier bags woven together to make a sheet, paint pots stripped back to their metal and used as plant pots, shopping bags stitched together from old rope and a hundred other improbable creations. We had around an hour of free time to explore the little backstreets and purchase a moderate amount of shit with which to fill up our spare room before heading to a local restaurant for a buffet meal with one included soft drink no less. There was no organised seating for this and the group were left to wander and find our own seating which is how we found ourselves sharing a table with a young couple who were independently travelling in the country and who were only too keen to share their views on how inferior our package holiday was,

"Well we did consider a package holiday but we wanted to experience the REAL Morocco you see." the pretentious young man informed us with his girlfriend's enthusiastic agreement.

"Package holidays are so privileged aren't they, it keeps you so isolated from the REAL people, not like the hostels where we're staying." This particular comment nearly caused me to sustain a serious eye rolling injury. I didn't like to point out that we were still both in the same place now, that they were seeing the same things that we were seeing and eating their meal in the same place that we were eating ours. The only difference is that we would be retiring to a nice hotel with a comfortable room and a bar that serves cocktails while they would be sleeping on the floor of a hut somewhere after shitting in a hole that they dug themselves. Now please don't misunderstand me, there is absolutely nothing wrong with staying in a hostel, sleeping on a camp bed or travelling on a budget. We have been there and have had to make do when money has been short. We have stayed in some right dumps over the years and that's fine but pretending that you are somehow morally superior because you are choosing to be with the REAL people is patronising and is frankly going to piss me off. The only plus was talking about privilege and REAL people did remind me of a quote that always makes me laugh. It's from Selma Hayek in an interview with the Times Magazine;

"I'm a very good step mum. I always wanted more children, but I couldn't have another after Valentina. You have to work very hard to please them all. If you are making pizza, there is one who doesn't like cheese, and another who hates tomato. Our chef sometimes looks so downhearted. He's always saying, 'Madam, what are we going to do?'"

That quote makes me laugh every time I read it but I'm sure our earnest young dinner companions would find it most distasteful and would thoroughly disapprove of someone so unashamedly not REAL!

After a little free time in which we did nothing of any note and an uneventful coach journey we found ourselves back at our nice hotel in Agadir where we could enjoy a nice meal, some cocktails and a comfortable bed. We were given tickets when we arrived at the hotel for five themed restaurants that were sited throughout the complex comprising Italian, Indian, Japanese, Mexican and Brazilian cuisine. There was also the main restaurant which served the English and Local dining choices and which was available to you at all times, the themed restaurants could only be dined in once and no more during your stay and only upon presentation of your ticket. These unreasonable rules had resulted in an underground trade developing amongst the English-speaking guests who were all happily bartering and swapping their tickets with each other so they could dine wherever they liked. I personally was more than happy to give up the Japanese and Brazilian tickets in return for one Italian meal and that night we again dined on a starter of tomatoes and mozzarella followed by a steak with peppercorn sauce, double fried chips and mushrooms with a small side salad, and cheesecake to finish it all off. And so it was I found myself an hour or so later sat alone on the toilet back in our room while Shaun reclined on the bed to let his dinner go down. Back at home it is my custom to take my smart phone with me or at least a book as frankly I find going to the toilet pretty boring otherwise. Sometimes the Youtube videos of people falling over have been so diverting that a good half hour will have passed before I rise from the seat and discover that my legs are now useless and that in a few seconds time I will be in the grip of some killer pins and needles. In Morocco there was no such distraction, bringing a book was an option but it hadn't occurred to me and so it was that sitting there with nothing much to do my eyes began to wander around my surroundings until my gaze fell upon the bidet some two feet to my left-hand side. Just in case you have never heard of this Wikipedia describes a bidet as something

> 'primarily used to wash and clean the genitalia, perineum, inner buttocks and anus... despite appearing similar to a toilet, a traditional bidet may be more accurately compared to a sink.'

Put bluntly you sit on it and turn on the tap which will direct water in the direction of your backside thus washing away any lingering remains of your recent bowel movement. A replacement for toilet roll basically. Now I have seen these before but being thoroughly English have never actually considered using it although on this occasion and being somewhat bored my curiosity was aroused. Could such a contraption really provide the level of cleanliness that was required at these times. Would the water flow be up to the challenge I wondered and in a spirit of inquiry I reached over, while still seated on the toilet, and with one smooth twist of the wrist turned the tap on full. Now in my head what should have happened was that a small flow of water would trace a gentle arc from the back of the bowl to the front, something like a large drinking fountain of the sort you used to get in school, but the reality was somewhat different. A jet of water reminiscent of a burst water main rose upwards and outwards, crossing the bathroom and impacting the opposite wall some six feet away where it began to splatter in every conceivable direction. The force was so staggeringly unlike what I was expecting that for several seconds I found myself sat open mouthed watching the watery mayhem unfold in front of me. Composing myself from the shock I quickly reached back over and turned the tap off but it was too late… the damage was done and approximately a thousand litres of water had been let loose around me. The room now had the appearance of a scene from the Poseidon adventure only with more water. On the walls, the ceiling, and from the light fittings a million little droplets sparkled in the light and it was of sufficient depth around my feet that ripples were clearly visible on its surface when I moved my toes.

"Shit" I said and really meant it.

"Is everything all right in there?" asked Shaun with a raised voice from his position on the bed, his sixth sense for detecting my stupidity clearly twitching.

"Fine, Fine. I'm just having a quick shower" was my not entirely untruthful reply after which I spent some time staring at the aftermath and wondering how to deal with it. Using the towels to soak it up was the only option and I set to work with one of the bath towels laying it out across the floor and then picking it up and wringing it out over the bath and after a mere fifteen minutes of effort the water levels had visibly receded, a quick wipe of the walls and light fittings with one of the hand towels and the room was back to normal. Mustering the most innocent look possible I emerged into the bedroom and Shaun passed me on his way to use the now vacant bathroom.

"What the fuck's happened in here?" he immediately asked on entering the room. Obviously my cleanup operation was not nearly as effective as I had imagined. It was impossible to maintain a straight face and in between snorts of laughter I outlined my investigations and its consequences and it earned me the single solitary admonition of;

"Twat."

The next day was to be a lazy day for us. We had considered a day on the beach but we soon discovered that one downside of being on the Atlantic coast was a persistent wind with strong gusts that made the beach a less than pleasant prospect with handfuls of sand being blasted into every facial orifice and somehow finding its way into every item of clothing. We instead opted for a day by one of the many pools in the hotel complex where we were also on an all-inclusive package so drinks and snacks would be close at hand and free. There are plenty of people that look down on an all-inclusive option which is something that I don't understand. A four-star hotel is a four-star hotel whether its all-inclusive or not and throughout the day you can get a soft drink or an alcoholic beverage for free as required and nip off to get a little snack as and when you want. Soft drink prices in most places are now frankly so exorbitant that getting them for free is almost worth the cost of all-inclusive on its own. If in the evening your tastes are a little more a'la carte then there is nothing to stop you leaving the hotel and finding a nice local restaurant to suit your tastes. Having stayed in a wide variety of hotels across six continents I can tell you with authority that all hotel food is a little bit crap anyway so take my advice and book all-inclusive which will be perfectly comfortable, and then go out for dinner.

We were to spend that day cocooned in the comfort of our hotel, sheltered from the winds by the high walls and a world away from the harsh Sahara which was less than half a day's travel away. The Sahara has one of the harshest climates in the world and the pattern of the winds I have just mentioned contribute to that. Located in the trade winds belt the region is subject to winds that are frequently strong and that blow constantly from the northeast of the northern hemisphere and the southeast in the southern hemisphere, and are created by a subtropical high-pressure cell and an equatorial low-pressure cell. They are known as the Trade Winds as they are so reliable that in the days of sail boats trade routes could reliably be planned along their path. The northern slopes of the Atlas Mountains trap most of the moisture from winds blowing inshore from the Mediterranean Sea which makes them somewhat more lush and green and leaves only dry and increasingly warmer air blowing into the interior. When the winds are reversed, which they can be and blow outwards from the Sahara they are given new names and these names in my opinion are wonderful. The sirocco, simoom, and harmattan are but three of them and in my mind conjure up exotic images of foreign lands rather than thoughts of dry, desiccated and dust laden winds whipping over a barren desert.

The Sirocco wind is a name given to any south-easterly or westerly winds that originate in the hot dry desert air of North Africa, and which then blow upwards into the Mediterranean which you might think would bring some lovely weather with it, but you would be wrong. On the north coast of Africa it brings dry and dusty conditions but as it crosses the Mediterranean sea it generates strong storms, even hurricane conditions and picks up huge amounts of moisture some of which will be dumped as heavy rainfall on southern Europe. In Italy it is known as the 'blood rain', so called because of its red colour resulting from the mixture of water with red dust from the desert. If you didn't know what was happening it would seem like a biblical plague was being visited upon your town. This same wind is known as the Khamseen where it blows across Egypt, so called as the word means fifty and the wind is said to blow for fifty days and it is also known as the Gibli in Libya and Xlokk in Malta and is often associated with poor health and damage to mechanical equipment, neither of which are desirable.

The Simoom describes those winds that head to the east and blow across Israel, Jordan, Syria and the Arabian Peninsula and the last wind mentioned known as the Harmattan describes those winds still originating from the same place but which then head in the opposite direction, passing over West Africa and out into the Gulf of Guinea.

These winds due to where they originate are always dry and hot and can frequently carry large amounts of sand and dust. If the winds are particularly vigorous they can carry all the way to the United Kingdom where we will get some pleasant weather and a fine layer of sand will be deposited on our parked cars and nowhere else!

Climate change is having a substantial and devastating impact on our climate and weather systems and the Anti-Atlas region of southern Morocco is being particularly hard hit suffering from a sustained drought. However, a project called Dar Si Hmad has been set up and is seeking to utilise the ocean winds combined with the heavy fogs typical of the region to address this problem. De-population of the area has escalated in the last few years as people have been forced to flee because of the lack of water leaving behind the poorest in the country who are disproportionately women, children and the elderly. They face a trek of many hours every day to find wells than can still meet their needs and so a large international effort is being made to find a better solution. The Fog Catchers that they are developing was inspired by the beetles of the Namib desert to the southwest of Africa. Being one of the hottest places on the planet the only source of water for the beetles comes from a fine morning fog which travels across the desert at almost gale force speeds. The speed at which the fog travels means that it won't stick to and condense on most surfaces except for the Stenocara beetle who's back is perfectly shaped with ridges and furrows which capture the moisture from the air, condenses it into water droplets and then allows it to run down over its back and straight into its mouth. Isn't nature simply amazing sometimes, seemingly with an answer to any problem that you care to think of. Fog harvesting as a technology has actually been around since the 1980's and began in South America but it has now spread from Chile and Peru to places in Ghana, South Africa, Eritrea and to California where drought conditions are bordering on becoming a national emergency. The original projects contained a series of nets which were found to be reasonably effective in capturing the water but the new generation of projects have been inspired by the beetles remarkable contours and the Moroccan project is hoping to incorporate these new lessons into its technology. In 2005 the first efforts began to bring the project here and on World Water Day 2015 the project became fully active after four years of testing. The project consists of a series of nets set at an altitude of 4000 feet which allow the wind pushed fog to be captured and condensed capturing an average of 6000 litres of water every day. It is filtered to take out any impurities and then piped to hundreds of residents in five local villages. The director of Dar Si Hmad, Jamila Bargach, gave an interview to CNN in which he pointed out that;

> "The fog is pushed by the winds from the ocean and is trapped by the mountains, it's stuck here, so it's easy to empty it of its water," adding that the

mountains are draped in fog for an average of 140 days a year. Not only is it effective it is also cheap, much cheaper than the alternative in fact. If the wells that these people rely on run dry then bringing in tankers of water costs £3 to £5 per ton, whereas the fog catchers which provide clean water straight to the house comes in at less than 50p a ton. Recognising its contribution to dealing with the challenges of climate change the United Nations awarded the project the 2016 Momentum for Change award and it was even showcased at the UN's climate change conference in Marrakech. Dr Bargach has said that people from the local population have experienced positive life changing consequences as a result of their work with one resident saying,

"We were like slaves, and now we're free."

Even though the people are poor everyone pays their bills on time for the water as they know that the money goes straight back into the maintenance and expansion of the system, and it does require a lot of maintenance. The nets are regularly battered by winds of over 70mph and require constant care and attention to keep them working at peak efficiency, although a German company is providing new technology called Cloudfisher to replace the current FogQuest technology which will double the water yield and which they claim requires minimal maintenance. That will make it more reliable and even better value for money and I just hope that they are proved to be right.

The winds and the moisture that they bring also contribute to the country's wellbeing in another very positive and important way and that is in wine production. Now if you are still with me this far into the book then you may have noticed that myself and Shaun do enjoy a glass or two of an evening. Whether that be from a carafe on a beach in Corfu, an expensive bottle in a refined Italian restaurant or my personal favourite, while sat in my underpants at home watching old episodes of Poirot.

Wine production in Morocco has a long history stretching back to Phoenician settlements some three millennia ago and indeed in the 1950's they were the third largest wine exporting nation on earth which was to me surprising as I have never seen a Moroccan wine for sale outside of Morocco. Alas, when the country gained independence there was something of a vogue for the nationalisation of industries and unfortunately Morocco was no exception so the highly successful vineyards were taken into public ownership where they could better serve the public and thrive under the enlightened leadership of the political elites. In reality of course, as with all nationalised industries, it collapsed under the dead hand of the state. Protected from competition and the innovation which it brings the industry began a dramatic slide into obscurity with the amount of land dedicated to wine production collapsing from over fifty thousand hectares in the 1950's to just over twelve thousand in 2015. Robert Joseph, the founder-editor of wine magazine and two times winner of the Glenfiddich wine writing award does say in his book 'The Complete Encyclopedia of Wine' that most of the varieties of grape lost in this time were Carignan, Aramon and Alicante Bouschet whose disappearance he describes as being no great loss to the world of wine. Ouch!

In his own words,

"The focus now is on growing Rhone and Bordeaux varieties on hillside sites that are cooled by the Atlantic breeze. Wineries like the Domaine de Sahari are proving what can be done here by making good Bordeaux style reds, while Sincomar produces reasonable wines using Rhone varieties, including the memorable named Rabbi Jacob."

The interest of French companies who are now heavily investing and helping the industry reestablish itself is down to the efforts of King Hassan II who during the 1990's decided that he wanted to recapture the country's former glory as a wine producer. He had studied in Bordeaux as a young man and had connections he was able to call upon for advice in his project and as of 2016 he can say his efforts have been a sterling success. The eight established vineyards are now employing over twenty thousand people and production has hit nearly 35 million bottles. They are in second place behind South Africa as the largest wine exporter in Africa and with the focus, investment and passion they are bringing to the game it seems likely that they will close that gap over the coming years. Morocco exports 52 thousand hectolitres to South Africa's 4 million! The types of grape that you can grow depend greatly on the local climate conditions and the moisture trap of the Atlas Mountains, the drier conditions towards the Sahara and the Atlantic and Harmattan winds produce enough variation of climate conditions for them to be growing several international award winning varieties including Syrah, Chardonnay, Sauvignon and Viognier. What makes this story even more surprising is that this industry is flourishing against a background of social conservatism that frowns on the consumption of alcohol. The law of the land in fact prohibits the sale of alcohol to any Muslim and many of the larger chain stores will stock no intoxicating liquors on their shelves. The demand they have is almost entirely dependent on a thriving tourist trade and the sales to them through hotels, bars and restaurants, selling to non-Muslims while certainly not being applauded or promoted is at least tolerated. This group of entrepreneurs are certainly making the most of the domestic opportunities as well as developing their export sales with a higher quality of wine more suited to making a journey across continents. The name that I found crops up most regularly when looking into wine production here has been Les Celliers de Meknes wine producers and particularly their Chateau Roslane vineyard which is spread across the temperate plains at the foot of the Atlas Mountains. A visit to their website will proudly boast of this being 'Morocco's first viticultural "chateau" situated in… Les Coteaux de l'Atlas associating history, modernity, tradition and sophistication.' You certainly can't say that they are lacking in ambition and they have set themselves the almighty challenge of industrialising their production process while not compromising on the quality of their product. Their website proudly boasts of a 70,000 hectolitre air-conditioned cellar, coaxial heat exchangers, underground ageing cellars featured with constant temperature and humidity control, 3000 oak barrels and 3 million laid bottles, epoxy coated vats with nitrogen injection, earth filters, tartaric wine stabilization and all of this overseen by an oenologist cellar Master and a team of mirco-biologists with their own state of the art laboratory facilities. They boast no less than 16 varieties of wine produced for export, and list pages and pages of the distributors they use spanning the whole globe. I have absolutely no idea what any of those processes involve or what the point of them is but they are clearly important to the finished product and I imagine that vineyards everywhere must have operations of similar scope and complexity to this one. Perhaps next time a bottle of £5 wine is opened I shall spare a thought for how much effort by so many people has gone into its production, or maybe I will be so focused on Poirot that it won't even occur to me. Who knows?

We had now reached that horrible point of any holiday where it seemed as though it was all but over and instead of thinking 'ah, another 5 days of relaxation' it had turned into 'we go home the day after tomorrow' and our thoughts were turning to collection times and packing our bags, but we did have one more full day of distraction between us and the flight home and that was a full day exploring the city of Marrakech.

Marrakech lies in a spacious plain called the Blad el Hamra or colloquially as 'the Red' with the foothills and then the snowcapped peaked of the Atlas mountains rising up and providing an attractive backdrop. The primary building material is red sandstone with very few buildings rising more than a couple of floors and resulting in the nickname of the 'ochre city' or simply the 'red city'. The centre is encompassed by great city walls punctuated with gates for access that easily earn the description of monumental and the whole area is also surrounded by, and interspersed with beautiful gardens and parks which do mitigate the neglected and run down state that much of the city finds itself in today. The city ranked as one of the most important in Islam during its early centuries with the development of not only spectacular places of worship like the mosque of Koutoubiya with its dominating 221-foot-high tower but also many religious scholars were produced by the schools in the town. Today it is still one of the most important cities of Africa, not only as a thriving tourist destination providing cold hard currency from foreign visitors but also as a hub for trade from across the continent. Like many of the cities in this part of the world there is a central Medina which is a thriving market (or Souk) contained within the old walls of the fortified city. Marrakech boasts the better part of two dozen souks selling anything from local craftwork, paintings, carpets, jewellery and so on up to microwaves, blenders and T.V. sets. There can be few places that offer such a crowded, noisy, colourful, smelly blend of stimulation. The whole place assaults the senses with sights and sounds intruding upon you from every direction. It is also one of the main centres of the illegal wildlife trade and acts as a hub where the poachers from across Africa can readily find middle-men to sell on their dubious goods to international buyers. As you walk around the markets it will take little effort to happen across Ivory products, leopard skins, hyena skins and snake products most of which are from protected species and many of which are on the endangered species list. The trade in live animals is also well established I'm sorry to say with traders offering up tortoises, Barbary Macaques and a variety of snakes amongst other things. It is a shaming fact that much of the demand for these creatures comes from the visiting tourists who will often purchase and smuggle these creatures back home with little thought for the damaging consequences they are inflicting both upon the individual animal as well as the species as a whole. Aside from the animals for sale you will also find a thriving trade in picture taking with many snake charmers enticing their cobras to perform just a few feet away from the passing crowds, and parrots and monkeys on leads being encouraged onto any vacant passing shoulder with demands of payment made for a photo before the creatures will be removed. We found their selling tactics aggressive at times with creatures sometimes placed onto your shoulder without your knowledge or permission and then what I would describe as demands with menaces being made. As luck would have it I can be a gigantic arsehole at times and I don't intimidate easily so it didn't pose too much of a problem for us. A simple search of the internet with the words 'illegal wildlife trade Marrakech' will bring up results from the Born Free campaign, the rewilding foundation, the Barabary Macaque conservation group as well as hundreds of other conservationists and research papers all focused on the Marrakech outlet for the trade. In the next chapter on Kenya I discuss some of the issues and programs trying to conserve animals in the places that they exist but this city and the tourist and collector trade here are the other side of the problem. It is places like this that are creating the demand, driving up the prices and making it a trade worth engaging in despite its illegality. As well as criminalizing the trade it surely needs better education to dissuade people from making these purchases in order to remove the demand as well as tougher laws to punish the purchasers as well as the perpetrators who are doing the poaching.

The markets are like a labyrinth and it felt as though it was changing shape as we walked through it. Attempts to retrace our steps would lead us to seemingly new locations and unseen before vendors who would all swamp us, determined to secure a sale before we passed them by never to be seen again. With little sense of where we were and with no guiding plan we wandered until we emerged quite by accident into the dazzling spectacle that is the Jemaa el-Fnaa. This is the central square that provides a focal point for the city's tourists, street-traders, thrill-seekers, criminals, cooks, henna-ladies, acrobats, dancers, musicians, fire-eaters, snake charmers and story-tellers. The story tellers are a favoured pastime and there is a saying in the city that when a storyteller dies, a library burns as all the stories are kept only in their heads and are not preserved in writing anywhere. It is loud, very loud with individual musicians, singers and acrobatic groups adding to the noise of all the traders, and all of them competing to be heard against each other and against the background noise of a crowd of thousands. Every step you take will be met with some new experience, taste sensation, sound or smell and it can feel disorientating, one might easily loose one's bearings except of course you cant. You are in a square and with a look upwards the high walls and rooftop café's of the surrounding buildings will give you your location. The rooftop café's looked particularly inviting to us, a little oasis of calm up and away from the madness around us, somewhere to refresh ourselves with a little drink and possibly something sweet and sticky just to line our stomachs, but still with a front row seat of the square below and from where we could watch all the action whilst being calmly detached. You may have to queue, we certainly did, but let me assure you that it's most definitely worth it. The charming little roof terrace on which we found ourselves was long and thin with around a dozen tables, all of which were along the outside edge and provided a panoramic view of all the street theatre unfolding some fifty feet below. We could see the people, hear the music, watch the entertainment and keep an eye out for any passing celebrity for we were told that this city is a place that has them in disproportionate numbers.

The city has become something of a playground for the rich and famous with some famous residents including Gerard Depardieu, Richard Branson, Yves Saint Laurent, Kate Moss and Madonna amongst others. It has become a holiday destination for those with astronomical wealth and has been described as Monaco without the yachts.

Astronomical wealth of course means footballers these days and it has seen the likes of Gary Lineker, Zinedine Zidane, Ronaldhino and Cristiano Ronaldo. David Beckham is apparently a great fan and the locals claim it to be one of his preferred holiday destinations although I imagine he will be flying in on a private jet and be whisked off to some exclusive and private location well away from riff-raff such as ourselves. I imagine there is little chance of seeing him sipping a diet coke in a little roof top café or wandering about amongst the Souks but you never know. He chose this place for his 40th birthday celebrations accompanied by his wife Victoria and a host of guests including Eva Longoria, Tom Cruise and Gordon Ramsay. Musicians such as Usher, Lily Allen, Jennifer Lopez and Jose Carreras have been seen here along with showbiz celebs like Sarah Jessica Parker, Orlando Bloom and Francis Ford Coppola. All of them mixing with the uber wealthy and the politicians of course who crowd around the glitterati like flies around horse shit.

The hotel that screams luxury more than any other in the city is the famous La Mamounia. An expensive and rather chic hotel fashioned in a Moroccan style and close to the centre of town this has been a well-known haunt of celebrities, politicians and royalty. On offer are 135 rooms, 71 suites and three multi-bedroom riads. All will offer you an elegant retreat with intricately patterned wall tiles, gilded mirrors, wooden screens and colourful tiled floors. As you venture out from your room into the public areas you will find them spacious, minimalist in style, scented by cedar wood and cooled by gently babbling fountains. An exterior and interior swimming pool, a Spa offering local health treatments and four restaurants can all be yours from a mere £400 per person per night rising to what would be quite astronomical figures for the more exclusive rooms and for which details are only available by telephone enquiry. There is a certain level of guest for whom booking by the internet is not an option it seems.

Although football is not my thing, I don't listen to 'pop' music and am not enamored by Hollywood films, at least not anything produced in colour, there is still a bit of me that would be genuinely excited to see a celebrity. I can however honestly claim that the history of the hotel and some of its historic guests provide even more interest for me and perhaps none more so than Winston Churchill. He liked to 'winter' here to escape the chilly weather back in England and was such a regular visitor that one of the suites, his favourite suite, is named for him now. Unsurprisingly this is one of the suites that is only available by telephone enquiry, something which in my case is not worth pursuing as I point blank refuse to spend three month's salary on a hotel. Churchill was particularly struck by the beauty of the Atlas Mountains and, for those of you that don't know, he was an accomplished painter who returned many times to try and capture their beauty in his work. He believed that his finest watercolours were the direct product of the scenery he found himself surrounded by here.

In 1943 Churchill visited La Mamounia with the U.S. President, Franklin Delano Roosevelt after the completion of the Casablanca Conference in order for them to have some relaxation time and for Churchill to show off the natural beauty of the region to the President who had never visited before. The conference took place after the successful execution of Operation Torch which I mentioned earlier which liberated Morocco from the Axis powers and meant the planning could now begin for invasions into southern Europe from Africa. It was primarily a meeting between the U.S. and the U.K. in the persons of Roosevelt and Churchill along with the attendance, but little input of General Charles De Gaulle who represented the Free French forces who continued to fight for France's liberation from the Nazis from exile. Joseph Stalin, the leader of the Soviet Union, had excused himself from this meeting as the Battle of Stalingrad was at its height and he felt his attentions and energy were best focused there. Two things which stand out for me about the meeting are firstly that this was the first time that the phrase 'unconditional surrender' had been uttered by the Allied Powers. They stated without any room for misinterpretation that the war would only be concluded when the Axis powers had been utterly destroyed. There would be no bargaining, no deals struck, total victory was the only goal of the Allies in this fight. It marked a clarification and hardening of tone about their aims and ultimate goals and the way in which they would prosecute the war. Afterwards Roosevelt did clarify in a radio address what he had meant by this saying,

"we mean no harm to the common people of the Axis nations. But we do mean to impose punishment and retribution upon their guilty, barbaric leaders".

Secondly, as Roosevelt travelled to the conference he became the first serving U.S. President to travel by air. The plane in question was a Boeing 314 flying boat and so limited was its range that the journey from Miami to Morocco starting on the morning of January 11th 1943 would include stops at Trinidad and Brazil. The chosen airline was to be Pan-Am and the plane was known as the Dixie Clipper. Air travel was still in its infancy and was not considered safe for a President at that time so the planning and secrecy surrounding the trip was immense. Only a month or so later Pan-Am's Yankee Clipper was involved in a fatal crash in Lisbon, Portugal when the left wing-tip came accidentally into contact with the water while making a descending turn in preparation for landing. The resulting impact killed 5 of the 12 crew and 19 of the 27 passengers. If that had occurred before the President's flight I think it's safe to say that the Secret Service would not have allowed him into the air. The Boeing Sea Planes themselves were a marvel not only as a feat of engineering but in terms of the standard of luxury that they offered to their paying passengers. A standard which today none of our airlines come close to matching, even I dare say in their First and Business Class compartments. With a cruising speed of only 188mph journeys anywhere would take an astonishingly long time, at least by today's expectations. I described their range as limited which in comparison to now they were but at the time they were near the cutting edge of what was achievable, but it still meant stopping off at stepping stone airports along the way. This would make a slow journey even longer so to compensate for that the luxury offered was an order of magnitude larger with the offering of a 'one class' service for the super-rich travelers onboard. A lounge and dining area was available with separate dressing rooms for the different sexes so they could don appropriate attire for the silver service dinners. Chefs recruited from 4 and 5 star hotels only were on board to produce sumptuous banquets of five and six courses with a selection of complimentary wines from the finest cellars. The seating was easily converted into bunks after dinner providing a comfortable nights sleep while a second crew on board could take over and continue the journey while the first crew rested. Roosevelt had the great good fortune to celebrate his 61st birthday on board during the return trip and dined on a feast of caviar, olives, turkey, pickles, celery, green peas, cake and champagne. He got to slice his birthday cake while flying 8000ft above Haiti. The New York Times I am pleased to say reported that the Captain and crew politely declined the champagne and drank coffee instead.

Roosevelt had felt that straight after the conference he should have immediately returned to Washington to continue directing the war effort but Churchill was so insistent that he could not travel all the way to North Africa and back without seeing the sun set on the Atlas Mountains from a luxurious viewpoint in Marrakech that he eventually relented and agreed to spend the night there. They were to stay the night at the Villa Taylor in the Ville Nouvelle district (now the Gueliz district) a favoured location for wealthy French colonialists and in this case a wealthy New Yorker who made his retreat available as the American Headquarters during the War. According to the story and I am unsure how accurate this is the owner was a staunch Republican and was so appalled that a Democrat had slept in his bed that he disposed of the property and never returned. The villa includes a tower which rises five stories above the gardens and which had a clear view to the snow-capped Atlas Mountains on the horizon. Churchill made two of his staff form a makeshift chair by linking together their arms and had them carry the wheelchair bound Roosevelt to the top of the tower where he was positioned on a divan where from a reclining position he could watch the sky burst with changing colours as the sun set behind the mountain range. Churchill's granddaughter recounts in her book

'Travels with Winston Churchill' that Roosevelt was so moved by this spectacle that he remarked to Churchill,

"I feel like a Sultan. You may kiss my hand, my dear."

The last I heard the villa is derelict and nobody seemingly sees any potential in its restoration either as a home or as a tourist destination which is a pity as I am sure that I would not be alone in wishing to see it.

The very last experience we were to have here was that same evening as we watched the sun setting and the central square descended into darkness. As the light faded streetlights and lamps provided artificial illumination aided by the flames of the fire-eaters and jugglers with their flaming torches. The level of activity grew amongst the stalls in inverse proportion to the fading light and along with those we had seen throughout the day a whole host of new people now joined in the throng. Circles of drummers set up a rhythmic, pounding beat that reverberated through the air and your body without respite. Whirling dervishes in flamboyant costumes span for all they were worth, their clothing, bodies and heads following wild and seemingly unconnected trajectories. Balloon sellers began stalking any parents with children and horses and carriages began appearing in increasing numbers offering a romantic and lazy canter around the now brightly lit city under a clear, star filled sky. Not actually that romantic and lazy as the level of traffic also seemed to increase with lorries, cars, taxis, mopeds, bicycles, motorbikes and donkeys all trying to get where they were going with no concern for any other road users or any laws that should theoretically apply to their behaviour. Any horse and carriage ride would be passing right through this, hardly conducive to a romantic atmosphere. The centre of the square is soon dominated by food sellers, all setting up under the yellowish light of old light bulbs, cooking on portable propane gas hobs and creating a thick and richly smelling haze of smoke that drifts across the square. You can feast on broad bean soup, chicken tagine with olives and lemon, Sardines in coriander, parsley and cumin or maybe a meaty kebab of beef, lamb or possibly pigeon. Cooked vegetable salads with courgettes, peppers and tomatoes and served with a healthy portion of cous-cous compete side by side with selections of fish caught and brought in fresh from the coast that day. In order to wash it all down why not try a mint tea prepared to the local Touareg recipe, loading up your green tea with sugar and spearmint leaves and then pouring it dramatically from several feet above your cup to create a characteristic froth. If that's not your thing there are of course other teas, soft drinks and freshly squeezed juices, and I mean squeezed right then and there in front of you when you place your order from whatever combination of fruits take your fancy. For our last night in the country we could not have had a better place to be and it was with sadness that we eventually had to drag ourselves away so we could be ready for the next day's journey home. At least from home we could begin planning out our next adventure, Kenya.

KENYA

It was an overcast day in early October and there was a light but steady rainfall that was attempting to make the world and everything in it a much damper place. Myself and Shaun were stood in a car park somewhere near Gatwick airport watching an extravagant amount of steam pouring out from under the bonnet of the car. I had managed to limp the vehicle into our parking bay after a tense three-hour drive in which a bright red warning symbol had been illuminating the dashboard. Setting off from home in Derby we had a plan for our morning. This plan definitely included stopping off at a motorway services for a full English Breakfast and possibly a little last-minute shopping for reading material for the plane. This plan went out of the window when the warning light began to flash, informing me that the car was overheating. We were already on the M1 motorway and it was too late to turn back but fortunately I have a lot of experience with crappy cars and knew exactly what to do. With the windows wound down and the heating turned right up to maximum the engine temperature began to drop and I was able to relax, even though we were both now cooking! Stopping off didn't seem like a good idea just in case the car wouldn't start again so we just drove in a tense silence straight to Gatwick occasionally permitting a small amount of panic as we slowed in traffic and the temperature gauge began to rise and then relaxing as we picked up speed and it dropped back again. There was no time to do anything about the car when we arrived at the airport so we just left it where it was and decided we would phone for the A.A. when we returned. It would turn out to Shaun's considerable annoyance that me not getting the car serviced for the last three years meant the water leak from the radiator had gone unnoticed and this is evidently a very bad thing. Who knew?

This was not a good start to a holiday!

At least we were at the airport and ready to fly, in fact as we had driven straight here without stopping we were actually very early so there was plenty of time to get settled into our pre-flight routine. This consists of squabbling about who gets the window seat, buying things we don't need from the duty-free shops (like travel pillows that offer no actual support) and checking the information screen at thirty second intervals. A few years ago we did get carried away in a particularly competitive game of air hockey and when we emerged heard them making the final call for our flight, we were the last passengers to board and by that time of course all the bastards with oversized hand luggage had long ago filled up the overhead compartments. When you're as tall as me flying with your own hand luggage tucked under the seat in front seriously cuts into your leg room and comfort. As a result of this aggressive air hockey tournaments are no longer on the pre-flight routine so we generally stick to drinking even for the very early morning flights. After all being on holiday is the only time when its acceptable to drink first thing in the morning. Oh, and Christmas of course. Weddings as well I guess. Maybe on your birthday. Do I have a problem?

It is an eight-hour flight down to Kenya and the flight would take us over the equator for the first time and into the southern hemisphere which, you've got to admit, is a little bit exciting. We were going to be landing at Moi International Airport which was named for the second president of the Kenyan Republic Daniel Moi. He served as President from 1978 when Kenyatta (the first President and the man who led Kenya to its independence) died. Although it took him until the 1990's, and mainly due to pressure resulting from the end of the Cold War, Moi did introduce multi-party democracy to Kenya to replace the one-party state of the Kenya African National Union. Thanks to bitter divisions in the opposition Moi went on to win two elections in 1992 and 1997 and even though it's a long way from being politically stable and has had problems with intimidation, violence and the odd coup I guess people have had airports named after them who have achieved far less. The airport used to be called Port Reitz and was a base for the British Royal Air force for a long time but since re-naming it has been turned into a major air terminal and now provides a gateway for thousands of tourists visiting the country every year. Even after independence the newly installed President Kenyatta opted to maintain close links with the British even though we had jailed him for his political activities, and Kenya joined the Commonwealth and signed up to a long-standing military co-operation agreement. In any given year six British Infantry Battalions carry out training exercises in the Great Rift Valley where there is terrain that simply isn't available back in the U.K., Add to this three Royal Engineer Squadrons who carry out civil engineering projects and two Medical Company deployments who provide healthcare for the local people and you can see a mutually beneficial relationship has grown up from the one-sided occupation that went before. From the 1990's Kenya has been involved in numerous military deployments including peace keeping for the United Nations in places as diverse as Macedonia and East Timor as well as in some of their African neighbours. Since 2011 they have been at the forefront of the fight against Al-Shabaab insurgents in Somalia whom they border. Perhaps the most famous military operation that Kenya was involved in, although only in a supporting role, was the Entebbe raid. Terrorism is nothing new and back in 1976 on the 27th of June two terrorists from the Front for the Liberation of Palestine and two members of Germany's Baader-Meinhof gang hijacked an Air France flight from Israel to Paris with 250 people on board. The plane was diverted to Entebbe in Uganda where they were joined by three more terrorists and were welcomed by the Ugandan President and Dictator Idi Amin. He gave a speech welcoming them to the country and supported them with weapons and troops bolstering their position. 150 of the hostages were released on the 1st of July but 100 passengers who were Israelis or Jews were kept and transferred into the airport buildings. The hijackers sent out their demands for the release of fellow militants who were being detained by the Israelis with the threat that if their demands were not met by the deadline then they would blow up the plane and all its remaining passengers. Their demands came to nothing as at 0100 local time on the day of the deadline three Hercules transport planes landed after flying 2,500 miles from Israel and 200 elite troops ran out and stormed the airport building. During the next half hour all seven terrorists were killed along with twenty Ugandan soldiers and the Russian built MiG fighters stationed there which accounted for a quarter of the entire air force. Three of the hostages were killed but the rest were safely evacuated to Nairobi, Kenya where the injured were treated. The Israeli Prime Minister Yitshak Rabin said;

"This operation will certainly be inscribed in the annals of military history, in legend and in national tradition." and do you know, I think he is right.

We got our first glimpse of the country as the plane descended and Mount Kilimanjaro was poking up through the clouds below. The snow covered peak clearly visible to us in the plane but annoyingly almost invisible in the numerous photos we tried to take. Standing at 19321 feet it is the highest summit in Africa. This high point is known as Kibo but there is also a second lower summit called Mawenzi at just under 17000 feet, both clearly visible to us on our way down. Although Kilimanjaro stands alone it is part of a belt of volcanoes that run across northern Tanzania, this one just happening to step over into Kenya. It was a sight that we would get to see again from the bottom up when we were on safari. As we descended through the cloud cover the land below us became visible. It had a dark red colouring that stood out in the gaps between the lush green canopy of palm trees which seemed to stretch to the horizon in every direction. The soil gets its colouring from iron deposits in the thick clay called laterite and is normally very hard, rock hard in fact, as a result of the heavy rainfall and scorching heat of the region, but when subjected to heavy traffic or through droughts it can become a choking red dust. We would get to drive on some of the dirt roads of the Kenyan countryside and we would discover how uncomfortable this dust can be. At least the long journeys would give me the chance to read up on some of the country's history in particular its sometimes fraught and occasionally downright violent encounters with the British.

Kenya's colonial history under the British was decided during the Berlin Conference in 1885 when the

European powers all got together and divided up East Africa into their own spheres of influence, the indigenous populations opinion on the matter wasn't considered important. The British some ten years later founded the East African Protectorate which basically opened up all the rich fertile lands of the interior to white settlers, settlers who were given a voice in the government while the Africans were banned from any direct political involvement. Kenya ultimately became an official colony of the British Empire in 1920.

Towards the end of the 19th century a section of the coastline up to 10 miles inland and the islands of Mombasa and Lamu plus some other smaller islands were held on lease from the Sultan of Zanzibar and formed the Kenya protectorate which was distinct from the colony, distinct in the sense that they were seen to be different but not in any way which seems to have made a practical difference. I mention this here because it leads me into what I think is one of the most interesting events to take place here, namely the shortest war in recorded history. Relations between the Sultanate of Zanzibar and the British took a sour turn on the 27th August 1896 as this was the day on which the war would be fought. The conflict lasted just under 40 minutes and was provoked by the death of the pro-British Sultan Hamad Bin Thuwaini. The British did not like his successor Sultan Khalid Bin Barghash and thanks to a treaty signed a few years before they had the right to block his accession to the throne. Unimpressed by this Sultan Barghash barricaded himself into the palace with his personal guard and some volunteers from the civilian population. Altogether some two and a half thousand men decided to stand up for their independence from the British, the Brits were not impressed. In response they had mustered three cruisers, two gunboats, 150 marines and about a thousand loyal Zanzibaris in the port area of the city. The British ultimatum for the palace to be surrendered expired at 9am and two minutes later the British fleet under the command of Rear Admiral Harry Rawson opened fire. They quickly sank the Zanzibar royal yacht HHS Glasgow (a former British tramp steamer) and then they bombarded the palace which quickly caught fire, disabling the defending artillery and allowing the British to pretty much walk up and take it back. The Pretend Sultan as he had been called fled to the German consulate and escaped the country to German East Africa. It was all done and dusted by 9.40am. To add insult to injury the British made the local population pay for the ammunition they had used in defeating them. The victory reinforced the heavy British influence in the region which then lasted until after the Second World War.

We were clearly Empire building back then but the governments of the time had surprisingly little interest in East Africa and for a long time all involvement was limited to the coast and even there it was just viewed as a stopping off point for the long journey between the U.K. and the Indian sub-continent. That would change dramatically as time passed and full colonial occupation of the country would last up until 1963.

Back to the present and just before our final descent we were handed the paperwork that needed to be filled out to pass through the airport. The usual forms were in there for customs declarations and immigration control, but we also received a medical document relating to the control of swine flu. We were flying out just at the time when the near hysteria about swine flu and the threat of a global pandemic which might kill millions was in full swing. We were required to list any respiratory illness we had suffered recently and describe the symptoms. On disembarking from the plane, but before we got to passport control, we were met by some men in white coats and face masks and before we were allowed to proceed we had to be checked out and declared healthy. It was only a few weeks earlier that my doctor had informed me that to travel to Kenya I would have to pay over £200 for various medications and injections. Yellow fever, typhoid, polio, hepatitis, diphtheria, tetanus and malaria (a particularly virulent form that required a £60 prescription anti-malarial rather than the £20 own-brand from Boots), and by the way the tablets aren't completely effective so you had better have plenty of long sleeved shirts and insect repellent to make sure you don't get bitten in the first place. Yet here I was being checked to see if I had suffered from a cold before I was going to be allowed in! The various injections and tablets would keep many of the diseases at bay if we were lucky but we would still be left facing schistosomiasis, trypanosomiasis, Rift Valley fever, blackwater fever, Dengue fever and bilharzia to name but a few that have no vaccine. Perfectly normal for a tropical climate our doctor informed us, and with some intensive medical care we might even get to see England again. We might even regain the ability to walk and talk!

Still, it's their country and they probably weren't keen on adding swine flu to this long list of ailments from which they already suffered. Anyway, we knew we wouldn't be hanging around for very long as we had sent our passports away to the Kenyan Embassy and our visas were already issued. As the rest of the plane started filling out their visa applications and joined the enormous queue for their stamp we went to the desk at the end for pre-completed visas and went straight on through to baggage collection. We looked smugly at each other as we proceeded and behind us about 150 people were queuing at just two desks.

Our superiority and general smugness didn't last long however. As we stood by the baggage carousel the bags began to filter through. We watched all manner of bags of different sizes and shapes travel past us and then back down the other side but ours weren't amongst them. There were several false alarms as we convinced ourselves that our bags were on their way but on removing them discovered they belonged to someone else. Several bags came around with brightly coloured belts wrapped around them and we commented that this was a great idea and we would have to do this on our next holiday, which of course we didn't. The people who had been queuing for their visas came through a couple at a time picked up their bags from the carousel and headed off to the waiting coaches. We began to get a bit more fidgety,

"Ours must be here soon." I said. Shaun simply glowered.

We stood there for several more minutes as a steady stream of people sorted their visas picked up their bags and headed outside.

"I don't believe this" Shaun said with venom.

There were only about ten people left to come through passport control when our bags finally arrived. Shaun's case seemed in a pretty good state but mine had not been so lucky. One edge was covered in a thick coating of mud and in the middle there was a large footprint! I still don't know what it is about my luggage that seems to scream

'STEP HERE' to every single baggage handler in the fucking world. I thought about checking the contents but I had now reached the point of just wanting to get to the hotel and finding the nearest bar. We lumbered our cases out through the arrivals lounge and into the bright sunlight of the coach park at the front of the airport where we joined our coach and were seated with a bottle of warm water to quench our thirst. I was looking around and eagerly taking in my surroundings as well as enjoying the sunshine and blue sky. There were palm trees, bushes, flower beds and well-tended and watered lawns stretching into the distance, the airport building brilliant white with its red roof providing a back drop to this little unexpected oasis of nature in its grounds. This is a country with over a 1000 species of birds, two or maybe three or four times as many as Britain (it depends on which source you look at). My ornithological knowledge is feeble but I looked at them with excitement and wonder anyway. Nature seemed to have thrown off all restraint with regard to its use of colour in the local bird population. At home they all seem to be either brown or black and only an expert can tell some of them apart by fingering their cloaca or whatever it is they do. Here I was looking at a palette of blues, yellows, pinks, purples, oranges, and browns and blacks of course. The birds here also had far more exciting names to match their appearance; Madagascar Pratincole, Sooty Tern, Fischers's Turaco, Sokoke Pipit and Clarke's Weaver to name a few. Arriving in a new place for the first time always makes me feel this wonder and excitement, besides which we only faced a short coach transfer between us and relaxation which improved my mood considerably. We sipped on our warm water and waited for all the passengers to be rounded up and then we headed off on the last part of our journey. As we wind our way along the highways and byways there is a little time to talk about Kenya, officially the Republic of Kenya, its coast is on the Indian Ocean, its neighbours are Ethiopia, Somalia and Sudan to the north, Uganda to the west and Tanzania to the south. The country is more than double the size of the UK with a population about a third smaller at 39 million although it doesn't feel any less densely packed, at least not when you are travelling in the cities. Speaking of people the very first human beings appeared in Kenya and the great rift valley is regarded as the cradle of civilisation, all the humans of the world have descended from this small group and that, frankly, is no small claim to fame. The valley itself is a giant trough that runs straight through Kenya slicing it in two. It is contained by mountains to the east and an escarpment to the west. It is 80 miles wide in places and running though it there are a series of lakes and dormant volcanoes. Hot springs and steam jets can still be found giving a nod to the East Africa Rift Zone which is the largest seismically active rift on the Earth. The whole geology of the area has allowed the preservation and study of fossils which has provided a massive contribution to our understanding of Human Evolution and the fact that the area where human beings originated also happens to be an area where those fossils were well preserved seems fortuitous to say the least. All of that as well as wild animals by the bucket load and you can see why this place is such a tourist magnet.

Our thoughts were a long way from all of this as we were discovering that the driver of our coach was either psychopathic or was simply tired of life. If you ever feel like you need a thrill and parachuting or white water rafting no longer does it for you then I would advise you to take a drive in Kenya, but you better have strong nerves and no pre-existing medical conditions. The coach roared through red lights, cut in front of cars and in one particularly bowel loosening moment overtook a lorry on a blind corner on a bridge, I was picturing certain death hurtling towards us in the oncoming lane. As we completed the overtaking maneuver I let out the breath I had been holding and turned to look at Shaun who was fast asleep. He once slept through an earthquake in Greece so I suppose near death on the open road wasn't going to keep him awake.

We had to pass through Mombasa on our way which is a very modern looking city on first appearances but with a level of poverty that is truly appalling. Mombasa has been the site of a city for over a thousand years since a time when most of the great cities in the West were little more than villages. The traders here had links with Persia, India and China and the wealth of the city was legendary with the people said to wear clothes made of gold. We were looking out on slums filled with dubious looking stalls selling goods that our supermarkets wouldn't allow on their shelves, bananas so ripe they were black, potatoes that had sprouted and looked ready for planting again and a collection of tins bereft of both labels and sell-by dates. One stall in particular caught my eye as it sold soft drinks and was full of bottles labelled up as Sprite, Coca Cola, Fanta and so on but none of the drinks inside were the right colour, the Coke was yellow, the Fanta green and the Sprite brown, the people purchasing them didn't seem to care. In the middle distance were the towering office blocks of the financial district, providing as inappropriate a backdrop as possible, all gleaming metal and glass looking down on, or more likely over, the poverty that we were experiencing up close. The cities fall from grace was 400 years ago and was the result of the Portuguese raiding the city four times over a 90 year period, stealing the wealth that had been accumulated. At the same time they also found themselves under attack from the somewhat violent Zimba tribe who were happily working their way down the coast leaving a trail of destruction in their wake and this was all rounded off by the Portuguese taking over completely in 1697. This was only the beginning of the cities problems as over the next two centuries control was held by the Portuguese, the Mazruis, the Omanis and finally the British. The arrival of the British saw it become the headquarters of the East Africa Company and the area became the base for explorations into the interior. Its importance as a trading port, one of the biggest in Africa, has been retained into the present day and the harbour has been transformed into a large container port dealing with upward of 16 million tons of cargo annually. That modern, efficient place seems light years away from the slum that our vehicle was slowly picking its way through. As well as the traders and their clientele there are also a large number of pick pockets and opportunist thieves so we were told to keep the doors and windows locked. As we queued in the traffic you could see ne'er-do-wells sidling up to cars in front and trying the door handles to see if they could get inside. Not a week after our return a British couple in their 60's were stabbed to death in a robbery not far from where we had been. As we made our way through the streets the traffic got progressively worse and eventually it ground to a complete halt, we all began to strain our necks to see if we could see what had happened, or maybe this was just normal. After a few minutes the coach started up and we moved forward and now we could see the delay. To cross over the inlet for the natural harbour we would have to use the Kenya Ferry Service. There is no other way around if you want to get from the Airport to Diani where we were staying. There are no bridges and no other roads without taking a massive detour. As our coach sat in the queue for one of the ageing ferries to come and pick us up we looked out on large cargo ships moving from the harbour and out onto the open sea. They looked rather tranquil slipping across the surface of the water with seemingly little effort, unlike the area directly around us which could best be described as frantic. There were two solid lanes of traffic moving down to the loading area and two lanes leading away that would suddenly burst to life as a ferry arrived and unloaded. Off to both sides of the road were areas that were fenced off for the people who were travelling on foot. Quite why they bothered to separate them from the traffic with the fences I don't know as when the ferry pulled up all the traffic and passengers just crammed on together with people running in and out of the cars, in front of the coaches and jumping up on the sides of the trucks. The Health and Safety Executive back home would have had a fit. A large sign announced that the ferry had a capacity of 40 cars and 800 foot passengers but I counted 45 cars, 2 coaches, 3 lorries and at least 2000 foot passengers crammed on. Every spare inch of room between the cars and coaches was taken up with people, animals and baggage. Gangs of teenagers, women with shopping, people in suits, people in uniform, tradesmen with their goods, the whole range of humankind seemed to be represented by the passengers on this morning ferry.

While we were waiting to board the driver told us that there were four ferries operating here, two ferries that were built in England and two that were built in Japan and one of the ones from England was broken so that's why there were some delays, a little bit of national pride swelled in my chest at the thought that we are fucking up public transport abroad just as effectively as we are back home. As you queue you can look up at an electronic board that flashes up pricing information and boarding times followed by some adverts for a random assortment of products. An advert that caught my eye was one for washing powder, more specifically the OMO doorstep challenge which seemed rather familiar. A well turned out presenter knocked on the door of a housewife and offers her two packs of a rival brand for her pack of OMO. She then tests them out and decides that no, OMO is the brand for her. What caught my attention was that when she tested the brands the presenter stood and watched her scrubbing the clothes by hand! At first I laughed at the scene but then I thought about how much we take things for granted back home. It would never occur to me that washing would be done by hand although in fairness Shaun would claim that it never occurs to me that it has to be done in a machine either. After the adverts a big logo for the Kenya Ferry Service came up which then morphed into the following scene, a man was shown running towards the ferry on the dock and he slips and falls to his death under the loading ramp. The board then cut back to the departure times. Shocked and amused by what I had just seen I gazed at the board waiting for it to come back round again. After a few minutes the Ferry Service logo comes up and morphs into a ferry again, only this time a lorry driver takes his petrol tanker on too quickly which causes an explosion destroying the ferry and all on board. I sat transfixed by these curious information films which were showing us all the ways in which we might die during the next hour. It's certainly one way to pass the time.

Eventually we were to be loaded, the gates were opened and people and vehicles pushed forward intermingling to get on. We then had a very uneventful crossing and then an equal level of chaos on the other side as we all disembarked. And then it was on to the open road and a clear drive all the way down to Diani where we would be staying. Mombasa was left in our wake, a city that has less status since the capital moved to Nairobi, but one that retains an air of decaying charm in places, some of the colonial influence still apparent in the architecture around you, mixed with the very modern and the very dilapidated. After an uneventful journey we arrived in Diani and began losing passengers a few at a time to the various hotels on the way to our own. We engaged in the usual practice of remarking how wonderful all the other hotels looked so we could feel disappointed when we arrived at ours. Every entrance area seemed so grand and inviting, pools of exotic fish, grand canopy's, wild flowers and cozy looking seating areas with waiter service tempting us at every stop.

Arriving at our hotel we saw there was a plane white hut at the end of a drive flanked by palm trees. The hotel was somewhat plainer looking from the outside than the other hotels we had stopped off at on the way, against the mental checklist compiled at the other hotels it did not perform well, but inside it proved to be excellent. As we got off the coach some movement in one of the palm trees caught my eye and I saw that there was a large monkey not fifteen feet away watching our every move. The other hotels could be forgotten, we had wildlife!

The reception was covered with a roof but open to the elements around the sides. There was a fish pond, various plants dotted around as well as a fountain dominating the area in front of the reception desk. We stood quietly waiting to be booked in, passports ready, and the staff quickly and efficiently processed the new intake and gave us the information we needed about when the dining room was open and what time the bar would be serving until. As we headed off from reception we passed one of the bars and then the dining room, again covered with a roof but open around the sides, and then out on to the patio area. This looked out on to landscaped gardens that sloped downwards to the pool and the pool bar (possibly the most important hotel facility ever). There were several patio levels with tables and chairs nicely spread out. This would be where our evening meals would be taken on alternate nights, al fresco dining being an ideal way to get up close to any mosquitoes that happened to be in the area. The gardens were full of flowers like the bougainvillaea providing a stunning display to overpower the senses and all sheltered by a canopy of palm trees. In every palm tree there were monkeys. Our experience of these creatures in England is in the controlled environment of a zoo where there would be a wire cage between us and a fence a metre or so back to keep us well separated and yet here they were running around and mingling with the guests. There were three types of monkey at the hotel, these being the Vervet, Sykes and Colobus monkeys. The Vervet and Sykes were the most daring venturing into the guest areas and sneaking into rooms and pinching things if you left your door open. They were both quite small, about the size of a cat, and a light brown colour and it was difficult to distinguish between them. The Colobus monkeys were shy and retiring and seemed to keep themselves away from the holiday makers which was a bit of a shame as they were undoubtedly the most beautiful of the three. They were much larger and had very soft looking black fur with white patches and a very intelligent face that made you feel slightly uncomfortable when they were staring at you. We came close to one of them on the way back to our room one night as it sat on the staircase directly in our path. It was wonderful to see the creature up close like that and is undoubtedly one of the benefits of travel as you would never get to experience something like that back in England. Beyond the pool and bar there was a stretch of grass again covered with palm trees, their canopy providing much needed shelter from the sun, and beyond that the white beach and blue sea stretching out to the horizon. It was a scene that I could have stood and taken in for days if I had been allowed but we were freshly arrived and there was the room to find, bags to unpack and some exploring to do. We had been awake for just over twenty-six hours now with only some sporadic sleep on the plane to keep us going but the excitement of arriving meant that our bodies were happily pumping adrenalin about the place. We had Tea and Coffee making facilities in the room, or a kettle as it's more commonly known, and after mainlining some caffeine whilst unpacking we were ready for the rest of the day.

The room was basic but comfortable and most importantly did include a balcony with seating and a table. We were also spoilt with a sink each in the bathroom and a separate room for the toilet which I thought was terribly civilised, the only odd thing was the large glassless window positioned so that when sitting on the toilet you could make eye contact with anyone who happened to be on the walkway outside. The beds did have a mosquito net over them which added an air of exoticism and the only other improvement needed was a bottle of wine or two which was soon sorted. A quick shower to remove that grimy feeling of a long-haul flight and a change of clothes later and we were ready to venture out. We started in the hotel complex, a walk around the gardens admiring all the different plants that had been beautifully choreographed to stunning effect and supported by a watering operation on an industrial scale. Down at the pool we had a look around at the various facilities for polo, volleyball and water aerobics which we had no intention of using no matter how much pressure was placed on us by the entertainment team. A large water slide snaked down into the inviting looking water but which, I discovered, would quickly and efficiently remove several layers of skin if you were foolish enough to use it. We headed onto the grassy area that led to the beach passing by numerous sun-loungers which an early morning expedition would secure for us on the days when we wanted to relax. It was remarkably easy to spend eight hours lying there with a good book and a view of the sea, the pool bar close at hand to deal with our basic needs such as alcohol and the occasional snackette. At the end of this area there was a good six-foot drop from the hotel grounds onto the beach with a set of steps leading down onto the shining white sand. Shaun suggested that we should have a walk along the beach to see the surrounding area and perhaps have a nosy at the other hotels to see what they were like. It was as good an opening plan as any so we set off together down the steps and struck out on to the sand. Within two and a half seconds we were swamped by beach sellers. The crowd of people who had been sitting around chatting all suddenly turned and we became their focus. We were surrounded, some had jewelry and craft items with them that they wanted to sell us, some wanted to walk us to their shops that they promised weren't far away and some were trying to sell excursions from Safari companies. We politely explained that we had just arrived and wanted to have a walk down the beach and we were not going to be buying or organising anything that day. They paid absolutely no attention to this at all and continued to swamp us. Any one observing us from a distance must have thought there was a rugby scrum in progress. The activity was so intense that I had no choice but to walk forcefully straight forward forcing them to move out of the way. They were nothing if not persistent. Free from the main body of the melee we handled the few stragglers by being thoroughly British and refusing to even acknowledge their existence. Freedom found we attempted to put some distance between us and the sellers and headed for the sea. As we entered the water for a paddle we risked a backward glance and were relieved to see that some other poor saps had become the focus of their attention and we were not being followed. Unfortunately, the peace and quiet was very short lived as there were more sellers lurking around every corner. We paddled our way along the beach with the sparkling blue water of the Indian Ocean to our left and the palm trees and hotels over to our right. It was from these hotel grounds and from behind these trees we could see people appearing on an intercept course and no amount of hand gestures or feigning disinterest could stop them from making contact. We began to feel hassled and we became increasingly frustrated with this hard sell and the worst thing was how polite they are when they first get to you, asking if you're having a nice holiday, where you're staying, how long are you here for etc, but you know that any second they are going to try and sell you a hand carved monkey. Our technique evolved as we continued the walk, we tried ignoring them, we tried being firm, we tried telling them to 'fuck off' but nothing could stop them. We eventually turned around and headed back to the hotel forgetting that we had to run the gauntlet of the gang of beach sellers outside of the hotel itself. We were in luck, as we arrived they had snared some other poor unsuspecting sucker so we could sneak around the side and back to safety. We decided that instead of exploring any more we should perhaps find some sunbeds, get a drink and a snack and have a bit of a doze until dinner, and that's exactly what we did.

Diani was originally a coastal forest area but around three quarters of that has been lost in the last 25 years. The pressure placed on the local environment by humans is growing and the impact of tourism is having a profoundly negative impact on the local wildlife. The areas of forest that are left have become disconnected, existing now just as small clumps here and there making them very fragile and the wildlife now face problems they have never had to deal with before. The monkeys that have been resident here since long before we arrived now face challenges such as crossing the roads and electric power lines running through their trees. Finding monkeys injured in the road is now an unfortunate fact of life in this area as speed limits are not enforced and there are no street lights to let you see what is in the road. The power lines are also a real challenge as they have been put up through the remaining areas of forest but they have no insulation round them so if the monkeys climb onto them they end up with horrific burns. The monkeys do have some friends though called the Colobus trust which is a conservation pressure group that operates in the area. Its main aim is to protect and promote the primate population but that links into protecting the local forests and educating tourists and local people on solutions to reduce their impact on the environment. Their mission statement is: To promote, in close co-operation with other organizations and local communities, the conservation, preservation and protection of primates, in particular the Angolan Colobus monkey (*Colobus angolensis palliatus*) and its associated coastal forest habitat in Kenya. They conduct research into the primate population and their habitat, they operate a seeding program to bolster the forests, they run an education centre for tourists that is well worth a visit and they seek to educate local people on simple changes that will reduce their impact on their surroundings, and all this by volunteers who are completely reliant on donations. They have volunteers who go out and trim back the trees around the power lines so that the monkeys can't reach them and they also build monkey bridges across the roads so that they don't have to run the risk of the traffic. When you visit their centre they also teach you about how you should behave as a tourist towards the monkeys, something which I wouldn't have given a second thought. One of the worst things we can do is to feed them as this has nothing but negative consequences. Firstly, although we think we are being nice the monkeys see it as a sign of submission so if you then don't feed them the next day there is a good chance they will bite you to show you that they are still dominant and believe me you really don't want to get bitten by one of these creatures, all those injections you had will not be much use. Secondly the ready supply of food from the hotels has resulted in big changes to the local populations. The trust estimate that the Baboon population in Diani reproduce at three times the rate of the same species in Shimba hills reserve nearby where there are many fewer tourists and hotels. The Trust believe that this is almost entirely down to the ready availability of food from the tourists and it also means the baboon population is now much larger than can be supported by the natural habitat. Unfortunately for the Colobus monkey they cannot cope with human food so they are facing possible extinction. This explosion in some of the monkey populations and the growing number of tourists is leading to conflict between humans and the primates so they are working with the hotels to try and reduce this impact. The monkeys are viewed as pests and the hotels tend to hit them with things fired from catapults, set traps for them or shoot them, the trust are trying to find better solutions to the problem. They are also involved in a project to protect the local forests by getting the wood carvers to use renewable sources of wood instead of chopping down the slower growing trees, so if you are ever in Diani you should buy carvings made from mango or coconut. If all the tourists stop buying the carvings made from the coral rag forest then the wood carvers will stop chopping them down. simple. There is always a conflict in these situations where tourists choose to go somewhere because of the local environment and then are responsible for the destruction of that environment. If we can develop sustainable solutions to reduce our impact that can only be a good thing, and its certainly better than seeing these unique areas destroyed and turned into another concrete jungle.

We decided to spend an afternoon at the Trust to see their work first hand and we had to get ourselves a taxi as it was much too far to walk. We headed up through the hotel reception and out on to the front where several taxi drivers were reclining in their vehicles examining the insides of their eyelids. I sidled up to the nearest taxi and was just considering the politest way to wake up a stranger in a foreign country when some sort of sixth sense roused the driver from his slumber. He immediately shot out of the car firing apologies at us and opened the back doors for us to climb in. The inside of the car looked as though there had been an explosion in a brothel, and a fairly tacky brothel at that. Every surface was covered in red velvet with a white lacy doyle draped over any flat bits that could accomodate them. It was just a shame that he hadn't put as much effort into maintaining the mechanics of the car, shock absorbers and brakes being an optional extra apparently. Considering how hot it was I was also disappointed to find that there was no air conditioning, it was hotter than hell in there and yet the driver was still wearing a jumper! Opening the windows didn't help as this just allowed a blast of even hotter air to hit us in the face. The journey was several miles and took about half an hour, we clattered over pot holes, speed bumps and we swerved into the dirt at the side of the road to avoid oncoming traffic, especially the big lorries which give no quarter to innocent tourists trying to have a nice day out. We rounded a corner and had to slow down for a group of baboons that were just heading across the road, desperately scrabbling for our cameras which we had forgotten to keep at the ready, we strained our necks to watch them for as long as we could. It feels so strange to see these wild creatures wandering about in the streets, you might get to see the odd fox back in the U.K. but nothing like this. The baboons, a couple of adults and several babies kept our attention as we craned our necks to watch them until they turned into the surrounding trees and the cars gentle speed took us too far away from them. We arrived at the gates of the trust and turned into the drive heading for the main building which was set back some distance from the road. As we drove up we could see various cages and open areas either side but we couldn't see any monkeys anywhere. It was only as we were given our guided tour that we realised our expectations for the place were wrong. It isn't a zoo and the animals aren't kept for tourists to come and gawp. The cages are available to hold sick and injured animals if they are being treated by the vets at the trust, some of whom are volunteers and some who charge and the trust has to find the money to pay for. The centre is about education. It provides you with the information about the work they do and the wildlife and plants that can be found throughout the area as I have just explained in the preceding pages as well as a whole lot more. After a diverting couple of hours at the trust we took the taxi back to the hotel and decided to have some lazy time down by the pool, equipped of course with our new-found respect and knowledge about the monkeys.

As we are lounging on the sunbeds we look up into the trees and see a group of colobus monkeys heading over the side of the pool towards the rooms,

"Grahame, have you seen those columbo monkeys above us?" he shouted

"Columbo monkeys"

"yeah, look up there"

I looked up to see if there was a monkey with a shabby raincoat and a cigar but was disappointed. After saying this to Shaun he told me to go fuck myself and settled back down to his book. I found myself watching the monkeys and their progress across the hotel grounds. They are supple, agile creatures and I watched as they headed straight for the one room with an open door, shimmying up walls and jumping gaps that you wouldn't have thought possible until they disappeared inside. The scream that came from the room a short time later attracted the attention of everyone around the pool and so we were all looking up as the monkeys scattered and a woman in her underwear ran out on to the balcony waving the intruders away only to realise that she was now the subject of everyone's attention. Looking suitably startled by the situation she attempted a nonchalant walk back into her room. The excitement over we all settled back and carried on reading. That at least was the plan but the monkeys had other ideas. The Colobus Trust may have some ideas about how to keep the humans and monkeys apart to minimise the impact but it seems that nobody has bothered to tell the monkeys. Every time you take your eyes off your drink a monkey would start drinking it, every time you put a plate of food down there would be some little bastard waiting to whisk it away before rushing up the nearest tree and taunting you by eating your food while looking you straight in the eye.

We clearly couldn't travel all this way to sit by a pool and fight with monkeys so we decided to venture out and perhaps partake of a little light shopping. One of the first things to know about paying for anything in Kenya is that all prices are negotiable and you should never pay the first price suggested, to be honest you should never pay the second or third prices suggested either. I do find this bartering rather tiring although Shaun enjoys it enormously. Much better to find the fixed price supermarket, there is always one near you I promise, and although you might pay a little more for your food and drinks it still saves a lot of hassle and the prices are still cheaper than they are back in the UK. I might be able to barter with a street trader and save myself 10p on a packet of ready salted Pringles but I have to ask myself, is it worth it? I may well be in another country with its rich cuisine and a new plethora of flavours to tingle my taste buds but sometimes I just want a Magnum and a glass of Ribena. As it happened the fixed price supermarket was only about three hundred metres down the road from the hotel and there was a whole set of market stalls and other shops selling assorted crap masquerading as souvenirs, we would be spending a considerable amount of time here throughout the rest of the holiday.

Before we had come out on holiday I had spent some time scouring the internet for advice and tips on Safaris and a company that wasn't too far from our hotel had been highly recommended by a lot of people online. We had been exchanging e-mails regularly trying to sort out a deal. As it happens while heading to the shops we bumped into one of the sales reps from the safari company and he informed us that the guy I had been e-mailing wanted to meet up to finalise the details and we agreed to return to the front of the hotel a few hours later. We put our time to good use by getting some drinks and settling down by the pool and at the allotted hour we towelled off, threw on some respectable clothing and headed back to the front of the hotel. Our contact, whose name was Peter I now remembered, didn't turn up, instead a complete stranger pulled up in an unmarked van and invited us to get in the back telling us that he would take us to the office to make the arrangements. Oblivious to any potential threat I started to get in but Shaun was having none of it,

"This isn't what we arranged" he said

"It's alright" I said as I gestured for him to get in.

"You said the office was right outside the hotel"

"Well it can't be far, It'll be alright"

He resolutely refused to get in the vehicle and so I had to get back out again and apologise to the driver. Shaun was not happy about the situation fearing that we would be the victims of a machete attack for our digital cameras and walking boots. Fortunately for us Peter was terrified of losing a sale and arrived at the hotel within a quarter of an hour, he explained that his office was outside the gates of our sister hotel and I had just misunderstood when looking at the website. Shaun gave me a look which said everything I needed to know about my lack of organisation. They were excellent when we got to the office and gave us a map of Kenya and a host of safari options and after some serious negotiation we were able to agree on the option that suited us best. Finding two German couples who would share the vehicle with us dramatically reduced the cost and our departure time was set. We declined a lift back to the hotel as we were only a kilometre or so away and we thought a walk back along the highway might provide some interesting diversions. It didn't. We walked through the hot, now nearly midday sun, passing one hotel entrance after another, not a single shop or stall to be found anywhere. The only thing out of the ordinary was someone who claimed to be collecting for a Christian school but couldn't tell us what it was called or where it was. We eventually arrived at the shopping centre just short of the hotel entrance. Feeling very hot and sweaty we decided to get a drink and maybe an ice cream. The car park at the front had a number of large holes dug at random in it for no discernable purpose and crammed around the edges were a host of market stalls selling all the tourist crap under the sun. We could choose from sculpted elephants and giraffes up to five feet tall, hand woven rugs, key rings, chess boards, walking boots, hats, sunglasses, water bottles, magic charms, dye's, traditional medicines and a selection of herbs and spices. There was also a local artist who was desperate to get his artwork displayed in England. He was handing out business cards and offering big discounts if you would promise to take his work to an art gallery and give them his contact details. He believed that all the Brits were art lovers with money to burn and that would be where his big break would come from. Lots of people were making encouraging comments to him and taking his card away with them but you knew that nothing would come of it which seemed a little bit wrong somehow. This did not stop me making encouraging comments and taking his card when he collared me on the way past. We managed to get past the market stalls, turning a deaf ear to all the inducements, and got to the row of shops that ran along the back of the car park, and a more useless host of shops I have rarely seen. There was a clothes shop charging about five times the price of the stalls in front of it, a couple of estate agents and a travel agent offering the same safaris that we had just booked but for a considerably higher price, but there was also the fixed price supermarket. We headed inside and were reasonably impressed with the range of products that were available, although in fairness all it takes for us to be impressed is to find Nestle chocolate and Coca Cola. We had a good wander round finding a section that seemed to specialise in selling outsized goods. The flour and sugar were in 10kg bags and the vegetable and sunflower oil were available in 10ltr tubs, this must be what the Hobbits feel like when they meet the big folk. We wandered around aimlessly for a few minutes and then quite by chance found ourselves at the freezers where the ice creams were kept. As we were there anyway we thought we might as well treat ourselves. There were two freezers which had two distinct sets of products in them. The first freezer in a prime location at the front contained a selection of very well-known brands which would have been reasonably priced if they knocked one of the zeros off the end and a second freezer tucked further back which contained the local, never heard of before, ice cream. We opted to be ripped off and phoned our bank back home to arrange a loan with which to pay for a couple of magnums. This exhausting spending spree out of the way we headed back to the hotel.

Dinner at the hotel was always a pleasant experience. On alternate nights dinner was taken outside in the hotel gardens. A makeshift kitchen was rigged up and all the food was cooked in full view and then served freshly prepared to the waiting diners. It was total chaos as it was not at all clear where you were supposed to enter this makeshift kitchen area or which way round you were supposed to go. Plates were scattered about liberally in large piles so you just grabbed the nearest one to you and then head off to find the food that you fancy. It was always dark by the time that dinner was served and the gardens had a wonderful intimate feel to them as you dined. The tables were well spread out and on several different levels leading down to the pool and the beach. You had a certain level of privacy around your own table but a nice atmosphere in the background created by all the other diners. There was waiter service for your drinks although if you wanted it in time to have with your meal you were better off getting it yourself, either that or you needed to leave a huge tip each time you were served then the waiters would be tripping over themselves to ensure the very best service. We gorged ourselves every night on a superb selection of food. Soups, breads, meats, vegetable, cheeses, pizzas, pastas and wines without limit. We never went to bed without at least a touch of indigestion. Our hunger fully dealt with we headed down to the pool bar and sat drinking till the small hours of the morning listening to the ocean lapping against the beach. We played Rummykub with another couple, Peter and Margaret, while getting increasingly sloshed and we kept saying sensible things about going to bed soon as we had to be up for the safari at five. We would then have several more drinks and another game of Rummykub.

And so it was that we both awoke with thumping heads at five, having only had a couple of hours sleep. We had booked a wakeup call from reception but I discovered on answering that I had no voice to speak to him. I croaked a response to him and hung up the phone. Shaun asked if I was alright,

"my throats dry" I croaked,

"It should be" he said.

Shaun then dared to accuse me of loudly snoring from about four seconds after my head had hit the pillow. This was very difficult for me to believe but Shaun was very insistent and frankly a little bit snappy,

"You should have rolled me onto my side" I quite reasonably suggested.

"YOU WERE ON YOUR FUCKING SIDE!"

I was clearly on the losing side of this argument, indeed the only other time that I can recall him being quite so tetchy was when he walked into the bathroom and found me vigorously scrubbing my scrotum with what I now know to be his 'face flannel'. Fighting my way out from under the mosquito net, which seemed a damn sight more complicated after only three hours sleep, I eventually got free and staggered in the direction of the bathroom. I could hear a noise in the background that I couldn't quite place and it wasn't until sitting on the toilet staring out of the window that it dawned on me that what could be heard was heavy rain and running water, a lot of running water. This brought back some bad memories as just a few months before while snuggled up in bed I had been listening to the sound of heavy rainfall outside, it was lovely and warm in bed and I was thinking how lucky I was not to be outside in what must have been a torrential downpour. After a while though my curiosity got the better of me and I got out of bed to have a look at this deluge only to find when I looked out of the window that it wasn't raining. The water that could be heard was from a burst water pipe in our bathroom and the entire room, landing, stairs and living room were flooded and I had been lying in bed listening to it for god knows how long. The living room ceiling had a very impressive bulge in it which would have possible fallen in had it not been for the pressure released from the two light fittings near the middle. The waterfalls from these two fittings were happily cascading over two pieces of our three-piece suite! Leaning in closer to the window I could make out rain falling on the landing that ran outside the hotel room. Here we were in Kenya in the middle of a drought and we had managed to book our safari to start on the first day that it had rained in months. This did not impress Shaun who's head was undoubtedly as tender as mine and after some low level whinging we decided to be positive and chose to believe that it would pass or it would at least not be raining up in Tsavo East National Park where we were heading. Feeling that a couple of aspirin might make my brain stop pressing against the side of my skull I attempted to open the aspirin bottle only to encounter the evil that is the child proof bottle top. These things may be no issue to a child who has all day free to experiment with them, but as an adult I simply don't have the time. As I cast around for a blunt instrument with which to smash it open it was snatched out of my hands by Shaun who then handed it back opened with the warning that I was beginning to get on his nerves. My survival instinct kicked in and we got ready in silence. We had seen plenty of films about safaris and knew that we required wide brimmed hats, cotton shirts and chinos along with a sturdy pair of boots so as to look the part as opposed to the t-shirt, jeans and trainers topped off with a baseball cap favoured by our German companions. Walking through the pouring rain and heat of a Kenyan October morning we headed up to the dining room where we were assured that breakfast would be made available for us even at this early hour. Anyone who has done a trip while on holiday knows that you should not expect very much from an out of hours hotel breakfast, cereals, croissants, cold meat and cheese is really all you can look forward to but our hotel surprised us. It was much worse than that. The options were cornflakes with hot milk, or dry toast as they had not defrosted any butter.

"You really shouldn't have gone to all this trouble" I casually commented to the waiter.

"no trouble at all Sir" he replied seemingly unaware of my sarcasm.

"no kidding."

I received a funny look for this last comment and then he wandered off to busy himself mopping the floor behind the breakfast counter. We munched our way through this meagre offering and headed out to the front of the hotel. The morning was dark, moonless, a few poorly spaced lights along the private drive provided just enough light for us to not see where we were going. The rain was not quite so heavy now but we still clung to the shelter offered by the hotel buildings and the trees of the drive. We waited at the security office which was only around ten metres from the road that ran in front of the hotel. There were no street lights out on the public road, just darkness and silence. I would keep wandering out to the road the closer we got to our departure time and looking to see if I could make out any vehicle in the distance.

"Any sign yet" Shaun would say every time.

"No, but it's not five 'o' clock yet",

"Are you sure?" and so it continued in a loop.

The road was very long and straight so I could make out the full beam of oncoming vehicles easily, vehicles I could watch for several minutes getting closer and closer until they arrived at the hotel gates and drove straight past me. I could then watch the red lights on the back getting dimmer and dimmer until they disappeared. After waiting around for what seemed like hours our 4x4 arrived at the actual departure time on the ticket. Our driver for the next two days got out and introduced himself as Mohammed and invited us to take our seats in the back by opening the door and nodding in that direction, the entire exchange taking less than half a dozen words between us. The two newly married German couples that were to be our companions over the next two days were already settled in the back. We nodded a good morning to them all and exchanged some small talk about how hot and humid it was and how we had managed to pick a day when it was raining for our tour and then we spent the next few minutes trying to get comfortable and figure out where to put our backpacks in a space that was patently too small for us or our luggage. We were both travelling very light with just our iPods, some books and a fresh shirt for the following day but it was surprising how big the bag seemed in the back of a 4x4 with four other passengers. Tsavo East National Park, which was our first destination, was along the Mombasa-Nairobi highway and so we headed off from our hotel back in the direction of Mombasa where we had come from just a couple of days before. Looking at the map of Kenya there seemed to be a road which would take us straight from Diani to Tsavo where we would be undertaking our Safari. Of course we wouldn't be going that way as that would be too easy, we needed to drive all the way back to Mombasa in order to get a permit to be allowed to travel to the Parks. The park is permanently manned and there is an office on every check point that you pass but you couldn't possibly get the permit from there, good grief no.

So while we wind our way back to Mombasa there may just be time to discuss Kenya a little bit more. The landscape that we would get to experience on our holiday barely scratches the surface of what Kenya has to offer. The country has the equator passing through it of course cutting it into two uneven halves. The north of the country has hostile deserts while the coast provides an ideal tropical holiday destination and then as you range inland you find the spread of national parks leading to the great rift valley, the origin of human beings themselves and where our ancestors may well have taken their first upright steps some 6 million years ago. The diversity of plant and animal life is unusually high and the country boasts six UNESCO biosphere reserves. There are over 10,000 species recorded but thanks to the 80 years of British rule many of the spectacular and arresting plants are not even from Kenya. The British abroad were keen traders and gardeners importing a wide and diverse selection of plants from poinsettias through purple jacaranda to roses and daisies. The seeds were brought from Europe, China and the Americas and artificial landscapes and flower gardens were created, altering the country's environment to the whims of the colonial settlers. Modern agriculture is still dominated by imports such as tea, wheat and potatoes. The need for all these imported plants is driven by the climate which is harsh and hot, driven by the need to survive the equatorial sun the local plant life is dominated by thorny scrubs, cactus like plants and ground hugging creepers, not the average Europeans idea of beautiful.

When thinking of taking a safari Kenya can provide the wildlife by the bucket load, the big five (Lions, Rhinos, Elephants, Buffaloes and Leopards) are to be found in relatively substantial numbers here, at least in comparison to other parts of Africa. The safari option that we went for however was dominated by the desire to see Lions and so we had accepted that we would not get to see any Rhinos or Hippos to my lasting regret. If you have the time and money you can of course get to see everything but we had to make the choice and Lions was the big one for us. Although, or perhaps because the hotel was very well irrigated so the tourists can spend all their time in an idyllic setting of flowers and palm trees the rest of the county does suffer from droughts and the country was in the grip of just such a drought now. Although we had experienced some rainfall at the coast it had been months since they had any substantial rainfall inland. When the land has got as dry as this it takes more than a light shower to replenish everything and we were warned that as we were travelling we may well see the carcasses of dead animals, some from being hunted and some from dehydration, and unfortunately the very first animal we saw was a dead elephant some 100 metres away next to a dry watering hole. When you have as much rain as we get in England it is easy to spend your time complaining about it, it takes something like the sight of that fallen, sun bleached carcass to make you realise how lucky we are to have it.

Anyway, I am getting ahead of myself as we have only just arrived back in Mombasa and are parked up outside the office where the permits will be issued. It is still very early in the day but there is a good deal of hustle and bustle outside the Ministry and most of the parking spaces are occupied with various safari vehicles, some more luxurious than others but all of them better than ours, with people of all nationalities stretching their legs and perhaps grabbing a crafty smoke while they have the chance. We got out and stretched our legs while our guide mumbled, "stay here."

adding another two words to the four he had mumbled in our direction over the last two hours. I am sure that there are many important reasons claimed for the permit, monitoring tourist numbers and vehicle types, planning service levels, determining the number of rangers required, calculating environmental impact and erosion rates etc. I am sure these reasons are claimed but as the only question the guy in the natty blue uniform asked was

"how many?"

and then charged an amount of money that reflected that number I couldn't help feel that this was more of a revenue raising exercise. This probably explains why the permits are issued centrally, if it was left to the underpaid staff out at the park to collect the fees then it's possible the number of people recorded as visiting the parks would drop substantially. Anyhow, we now had our permit and could at last take to the road and head off to see some big beasts. We drove and drove, and then drove some more and then for want of anything better to do we drove some more after that. The Mombasa-Nairobi highway went on seemingly without end and after a few hours we pulled over at a small group of shops with approximately two thousand lorries parked outside.

"You want to buy some water?" Mohammed asked

"We were told it was provided" I replied. Mohammed suddenly became very talkative when faced with the prospect of parting with some money. He was positively animated in his explanation of how it wasn't his responsibility and we should be sorting this out ourselves. Only a phone call to the office who told him they had agreed to provide the water silenced him. He stalked off to the shop and came back with a large tray of bottled water which was slung on to the passenger seat, we were not to get anymore conversation from Mohammed for several hours. We drove and drove and drove some more, you get the general idea, with very little to see apart from some isolated buildings and an awful lot of farmland that looked less than thriving. We did see occasional groups of livestock, some sheep and quite a lot of cows but nothing you wouldn't see back home. We did hear tell of a practice called cow blowing in this area, otherwise known as phooka or kuhblasen, whereby the local farmers force air into a cows vagina (or possibly its anus depending on personal taste) stimulating milk production and increasing its yield. This seemed highly suspect to me and in many years of camping on a Dairy Farm back in the U.K. I don't recall ever seeing Farmer John puckering up while kneeling at the back of Daisy in the milking parlour. It is a real thing though and as well as being practiced in Africa was also quite widespread in India at one time, Ghandi was appalled at the thought of it and refused to drink any more cows milk after hearing of the practice. I don't think it would put me off drinking the milk but I would certainly think twice about kissing the farmer.

After several hours of uneventful driving we finally arrived at the entrance to the Park which we drove straight past and went instead to a genuine authentic Kenyan workshop, or so the sign said. They certainly played the part well with a dilapidated court yard and various ancient looking men sitting around randomly hacking at bits of wood with what we were assured were genuine authentic Kenyan tools. I suspected that out the back somewhere was a large workshop with computer-controlled lathes that were knocking out the genuine authentic Kenyan merchandise at a rate that would keep up with the number of tourists that were being dragged in here against their will. We politely looked around, not wishing to offend, desperately trying to dodge down different aisles of the store to avoid the smiling assistants who stalked our every move. It was like being in the pac-man game and no matter which way we turned the ghost like assistants loomed up at the end of the aisle, duck left down an adjacent aisle but there are two more assistants looming up in front of you, and oh christ your route of escape has just been cut off, OH NO!

> "Good morning my friends, could I interest you in this genuine authentic example of Kenyan workmanship, only £200 pounds."

> "How much!" I exclaimed with raised eyebrows.

> "Just £200 my friends for a genuine…"

> "but its tiny" I interjected.

It was true that the workmanship on this small wooden elephant was impressive, computer-controlled lathes will do that for you, but £200 seemed a bit steep considering I have found larger objects stuck in my boots after a long walk. Firmly telling him that we weren't interested and backing away the price began to fall. As we gathered speed and aimed for the door the last thing we could hear was a voice in the background,

> "£30 and that's my final offer" he shouted.

We did not look back and instead retreated to the vehicle. The two German couples saw us and started to follow our lead but then disaster, one of the women was trapped by a sales assistant. The other couple made it to the vehicle and we all watched horrified as the lady's husband risked all by going back for her, luckily he made it out unscathed but her purse had taken a beating, this place could seriously damage your wealth! Mohammed got us out of there and as we pulled back out on to the road I hardly dared look back in case there was a salesman clutching a small wooden elephant running after us, his voice fading into the distance,

"Just £20 for this genuine, authentic…"

Relaxing after our ordeal the unfortunate German lady unwrapped some newspaper to reveal her purchase. None of us could help ourselves, our eyes were drawn to it in much the same way that you can't help looking at accidents on the opposite lane of the motorway. After a lengthy pause an unidentified voice said,

"What is it?"

Another long pause and,

"It's a giraffe" a voice said with certainty

We all looked at it…

"Or an antelope" the same voice said with less certainty.

"One. Hundred. Dollars" a shell-shocked voice said slowly and deliberately. This was the lady who had purchased the thing that lay before us. Decency reintroduced itself and we stopped staring at it, briefly made eye contact with each other and then turned forward in our seats again. I wasn't entirely certain but I thought I could just make out a quite sobbing in the back of the van as we drove on.

But now, look into the distance, the gates! The gates to the park right ahead and now we are driving towards them, no more distraction. The entrance looms up like the opening sequence of Jurassic Park and we pull up, parking alongside all the other 4x4's waiting to get in. Mohammed gets out and disappears into the mysterious recesses of the park office with all the other drivers and we all sit patiently inside the vehicle, no one has got out to stretch their legs here, the anticipation is too great, we want no delays, the other side of those gates is what we have come to see. Wildlife!

Tsavo National Park was established on 1st April 1948 and is about 200km from Nairobi. It is the largest National Park in close proximity to Mombasa and is popular as a safari destination. The park has an area of over 8000 square miles which makes it considerably larger than the more famous Masai Mara Park and also somewhat larger than Wales.

It is possible that sometimes people drive into these places and are greeted with sights that would make their socks roll up and down, this was not to be the case for us. We drove and drove and drove some more, can you see a theme building for this holiday? Anyway, after what seemed like forever Mohammed pulled the vehicle over, came around the back and opened the rear door. I wondered if he was going to dump us here in the middle of nowhere, driving away and shouting,

"Glad you got free water now" followed by an evil laugh, but instead he reached up into the recesses of the roof released some catches and then had us all push, this lifted the roof up off the vehicle, four legs extending out to support it which locked into place. We were then able to stand up in the back and get a totally unobstructed view in all directions. This resulted in such a high level of excitement that I squirted a little pee into my pants. As you can tell it doesn't take much to get me excited. The CB radio crackled into life at this point and Mohammed jumped into the driver's seat and the vehicle took off with the same acceleration as a jet fighter. I swear he drove with more speed on those dirt tracks than he had on the highway that had brought us here. We rounded a corner and there was another vehicle in the road, just off to the left were some antelope, perhaps 20 metres away and in the open. They were not spooked by the vehicles at all and we were able to drive right up alongside them and standing up got some photos to add to the album. After a few minutes we drove off and headed in some indeterminate direction. We pulled up alongside more antelope,

"More antelope" Shaun said,

"Oryx" said Mohammed, who came to life.

He told us how the Oryx is the name for the north east African antelope. They have a long-tufted tail and both sexes have long horns. We listened without paying too much attention and took more photos. After just long enough viewing them we drove on. I knew that Shaun was itching to see some big cats, it was the reason we were here on this Safari, and I didn't think that we would enjoy seeing anything else as much as we should till we had seen a lion. We drove for a while and pulled up alongside some bushes, Mohammed telling us to look carefully just to the left of a tree trunk to the side,

"baby antelopes" came a voice from the back.

"Lesser Kudus" said Mohammed, which it turns out are a different type of antelope which is smaller than the oryx. Over the next hour or so we were introduced to eland and gazelles, which are also types of antelope. We had seen four different animals that were all the same fucking animal. I know I shouldn't be ungrateful, some people never get to see these things out in the wild and I do appreciate that, but it was crossing my mind that a bit more variety might be quite nice and fortunately we were about to get it. The radio crackled into life and we pulled over near to an artificially created water hole. Mohammed told us to look to our right and slightly behind us, and there, distant but heading in our direction, were a family of elephants. I cannot do justice here to the feelings as that family of elephants got closer and closer to us. They got within metres of our vehicle and headed to the watering hole where the baby elephant waded in and the rest gathered around to drink. These were the famous red elephants of Tsavo and we were only metres away from them. The red elephants are not actually red, they are the standard elephant grey as you might expect but the ones around here cover themselves in the red dust that coats every surface. Tsavo spends most of the year dry and dusty but when the rains do come the park is transformed with a fresh growth of wild flowers and different grasses, there seeds lying dormant under the surface and just waiting for the life-giving properties of the rain. Although there had been some light rainfall the park was still pretty dusty. We can definitely state this as a fact as most of the dust ended up in our faces when we attempted to stay stood up in the vehicle as it was moving. We got to see a number of elephants during our trip and got within a matter of feet of some of them. The park has some six thousand elephants and given their size and general lack of stealth they are easy to find. Six thousand sounds like quite a lot but this area used to be home to over 50000 elephants most of whom starved to death during terrible droughts in the 1960's and 70's. Six thousand at least represents an increase from a low point in the 90's as the number had dropped considerably lower driven by drought, human incursion and poaching. Mohammed informed us that a by-product of the drop in elephant numbers was that the amount of vegetation in the park has increased as the elephants weren't there to eat it, and this had led to rising numbers of other animals as food was more plentiful, the circle of life in full flow. As we stood looking at the elephants Mohammed suddenly said in a tone that caught all our attention,

"Lion"

and pointed off to the side of the vehicle. We all ripped our gaze from the family of elephants and looked into the grasses where Mohammed was pointing. Everyone stared into the tall grass and not one of us could see a damn thing. Mohammed began pointing out markers,

"look at the termite mound, go up and to the left"
We saw nothing,

"from the tall tree, just in front"
We saw nothing,

"it's moving now, there, THERE!" he screamed, pointing frantically and virtually hopping from one foot to the other. We saw nothing.

"It's gone, it's gone" he said shaking his head and getting back into the driver's seat, a sense of disappointment settled over the rest of us as we all thought about what we had missed. What if that was our only chance? Was I looking at the right termite mound? Had I seen it and not realised? We would just have to press on and hope that we would find another one.

The day was full of other sights including buffalo, giraffes, zebras, elephants, antelopes, baboons and warthogs and then midafternoon what we were waiting for finally happened. The radio came to life again, we had worked out by this point that all the drivers in the park were on the same frequency and were all letting each other know where the best sights were. The word lions could just be made out and Mohammed again put his foot down. He bounced us down dirt tracks, overtook dawdling drivers, screeched us around corners and after over half an hour of driving at break neck speeds we arrived at a watering hole miles from where we had started and there sat right at the side was a lioness. As bold as brass you might say, untroubled by the growing number of vehicles pulling up alongside her. She must have been only 60-70 meters away but she was clearly visible and the camera was put too good use. We had really enjoyed driving around and seeing all the different wildlife in their natural habitat but this was something else. She was so elegant, majestic, powerful and close, right there in front of us. We stayed for a long time, just watching, she didn't do anything but that didn't matter, we still stayed just watching. The number of vans and jeeps around us grew and grew and eventually it came time for us to move on to give others a chance, which is only right but still really gutting. It seemed like a good time to get some food and we were, quite by chance, close to the hotel where our dinner reservations had been made. We drove a short distance and then made a sharp right hand turn on to a dirt track that was in an even worse conditions than the ones we had already been on and we started a long, slow, bumpy ride up a very steep hill. There was no barrier along the side and a steep, near vertical drop (or so it seemed to us) was only inches away but it was a drive worth taking. At the top was the hotel where dinner would be served and on entering we found that the dining room was quite small and cosy with only around twelve tables and one side of the room was completely open to the elements and the view beyond was the Park we had been in just a few short minutes ago. We could see elephants, zebras and some warthogs moving about as we settled at our table. We ordered our drinks and were invited up to the buffet to help ourselves. There was bread, rice and a pot of boiled chicken, pretty basic but we were so ravenous that we got through a couple of helpings. The chicken was quite delicious and certainly put the moisture free offerings that Shaun occasionally makes to shame. Our hunger sated we helped ourselves to some tea and biscuits and sat down to look out over the park for a while. It was only then that I noticed that a hill I had been looking at earlier in the distance was no longer visible. The sky had become cloudy and some might say that it was full of foreboding, not me of course but some might say that. It certainly looked full of cloud, heavy looking cloud, the sort of cloud that threatens flash floods and an interrupted satellite signal on the telly. There was just a sort of dullness in the distance instead of the view and the dullness was getting closer, the landscape disappearing behind whatever it was. Only when it was within a mile of us could you make out that it was rain, heavy rain. We watched it until the leading edge swept over us and the sound of it against the wooden roof of the dining room was deafening. Great gushes of water ran off the roof, overwhelming the inadequate gutters and splashing all over the place, including into the dining area, joining the rain that was being driven in by a sudden wind that had sprung up without warning. We backed away from the open side while hotel staff wrestled with some canvas wall that could be tied into place. Although the visibility was now quite restricted we could still see the areas of the park directly below us and we noted the warthogs dashing for cover under the trees, the zebras had done a vanishing act and the elephants didn't seem remotely bothered, except the babies who hid underneath the larger adults. We were glad to see the rain in some ways, knowing how desperate the wildlife was for this water, but... a little part of us was still pissed off that it was raining. We sat for about an hour watching the world drift by, or more accurately the rain plunge down and then as suddenly as it had arrived it had gone. The sun was back, the sky was blue and the air was still, although it did feel less oppressive than it had earlier. So it was back to the van for us and an afternoons sightseeing around the park. We covered a lot of the same ground again as well as some fresh areas and we added vultures, ostriches, eagles and buffalo to our list of sightings. Having only ever seen some of these animals in the confines of a zoo it took a little while for it to sink in that the animals all mingle together and aren't all off in their own little areas, Zebras, Giraffes, Warthogs all mixed in together, elephants wandering through a herd of bison and antelope drinking at the same watering hole as the lions, it makes you realise what a sterile environment the average zoo is. Late afternoon we headed off from the national park and faced a lengthy drive to the private game reserve where we would be spending the night. Feeling somewhat tired by our activities up to this point I decided that catching a bit of sleep for an hour or so might be a good idea but the journey was far too bumpy for that. The road gave no relief, not even for a moment, and there was self-evidently no chance of sleeping and yet still I persisted, as indeed did one of the German chaps who was sat behind me. We both gave up when we hit a particularly large hole in the road and we both engaged in some synchronised head butting of the windows, much too the amusement of our fellow passengers but not too ours. Eventually we arrived at Simba hills, the private game reserve where we would be spending the night. We disembarked and clumped through to the reception of the hotel where we went through the usual rigmarole of booking in, all the while looking forward to a cold shower and perhaps a quick lie down to rest our eyes and so it was something of a shock when Mohammed told us to head straight back out to the van. We looked longingly at the inviting pool, comfy chairs and well stocked bar as we trudged back out to the bone shaking heap of a van that was fast becoming our home. The sense of disappointment didn't last long though as it turns out that the hotel has two parts and the part we were heading too was spectacular. Salt Lick Lodge lay straight ahead. Raised up on stilts and surrounding an artificial water hole the lodge looked magnificent. A large central complex held the bar, dining room and reception and then the rooms fanned out either side in towers that stood atop the stilts. There was no pool, few staff, and small rooms but it was still by far the best place that I have ever stayed. On entering the reception area I noticed a sign which simply said 'the tunnel' and which included an arrow pointing down a spiral staircase at which point all thought of comfort disappeared as the need to explore took over. We dumped our backpacks into the room, jumped a mile as a large lizard ran out of the bed when I sat down, and headed straight back out to head down the spiral staircase. It led us underground into a dank and ill lit tunnel, working our way along watching for trip hazards, it brought us out into a circular area with a couple of windows at head height covered with steel bars, rather reminiscent of a jail cell. Looking through the windows we found that we were outside of the hotel and right next to the watering hole. The viewing room was dug into the ground and the windows were at ground level on the outside, the animals could walk right past us and even over the top of us. There were unfortunately no animals visible at this time but we would run back down here again later when a family of elephants came down and started bathing. We went out for an evening game drive and added a few more photos to the album, seeing everything promised on the game board at the hotel except for the cheetahs. Throughout the park there were a series of posts that were actually just large stones with numbers painted on them. Each day the game board in the hotel was updated and a list of all the animals in the park would have the post numbers written next to them where they had been seen. This meant that at a glance you could get out and stand the best chance of seeing the animals that you wanted. During our stay the cheetah only ever had 'try in the park' which did not narrow things down very much. The game drive over we retired to the hotel and changed for dinner which travelling light meant putting a fresh t-shirt on. We then discovered at the dining room that one of the main reasons that no one else was travelling light was that they all had formal clothes with them, not only were we the only ones without trousers we were also the only ones without a tie. Hanging our heads in shame we quickly loaded our plates from the buffet and retired to a table in the corner where we could look out over the water hole, a lone baboon being the only sight worthy of note during dinner. We hastily left the dining room trying to ignore the peoples look of disgust at these two people with such a lack of decorum and headed to the bar, which to our relief was empty. We debated what to have, which in our case meant arguing about whether to just get a glass of wine each or accept the inevitable and purchase the whole bottle now. We took the bottle and our glasses to our table and as I pulled out the chair something ran out from underneath, it darted underneath another table nearby and we both dropped down to our knees to see what the hell it was. It turned out to be a bush baby which is a small primate about the size of a cat which walks on its hind legs and has eyes about the same size as a saucer, it is, in short, incredibly cute and it appeared to be cowering, as I guess it is entitled to do when two men who are about 20 times larger than it is are on their hands and knees looking at it. Assessing the possible escape routes it bolted from under the table and using its incredibly powerful back legs made a jump of nearly three metres across a gap from the balcony to the roof of an adjoining building where we lost track of it, we hadn't even had time to take a picture of it before it had gone. We were unprepared, taken off guard, our cameras too packed away for easy access. This would be the last time that we would let that happen. After a pleasant evening of not saying very much to each other, drinking and watching the world in general go about its business it seemed like a good idea to get some sleep. To get from the central complex to the rooms you crossed some wooden rope bridges to the towers that the rooms were in and it was as we crossed one of these bridges that we saw the family of elephants underneath, we turned around and ran back to the viewing deck on the ground floor of the main part of the hotel and we were to be rewarded with an incredible sight, the family of elephants came right alongside the viewing area, we were no more than a couple of metres from these giants of the African plains. It is a site quite without comparison. Incredible, Breath taking, Astounding, Indescribable. Everyone should get to experience something like this, indeed if you haven't I would encourage you to put this book down right now and get down to your nearest travel agent. Sitting on a beach for a week somewhere simply doesn't compare. We would have liked to get some pictures with them but it was too dark for the camera too work and the flash was forbidden. There was a sign that said so in about six different languages including one that said 'fotografica flasha et non or else animals will scarperono' which sounded completely made up to me. We stayed for as long as the elephants stayed and I honestly couldn't tell you how long that was, we stayed until they began walking away, we stayed until they were out of sight and then we stayed some more in case they came back and then we went to bed. The elephant population is still under enormous pressure with their numbers falling from as high as five million a hundred years ago to less than half a million now. That pressure comes from loss of habitat with over half of their range being lost just since 1979 and from poaching for their ivory which has seen something of a resurgence recently. Despite a ban on the international trade in ivory African elephants are still being poached in large numbers and only about a fifth of their remaining territory is under any kind of formal protection. There have been some ideas on how to protect the animals in those areas where there are no formal arrangements. One idea has been to dye their tusks bright pink to render the ivory worthless. It was reported in the Daily Mail in 2013 that the Dinokeng game reserve in South Africa had put in place a project to dye the horns of all their rhinos in this way and to implant a tracker in the horn to keep track of it. Since the park opened in September 2011 they haven't lost a single rhino to poaching. There are however a lot of conservationists who believe that rolling this out across a wider population of rhinos and elephants would be impractical, expensive and stressful for the animals themselves. Another more controversial idea is licensed hunting. It seems strange that hunting and killing an endangered animal could help to protect it but there are many who are supporting exactly that approach. The money raised from the sale of the licenses could be used to support conservation efforts in areas which don't have the tourist income to support anti-poaching operations. By linking the survival and proper management of a species to the economic livelihood of the local population encourages a poacher turned gamekeeper outcome that could extend protection into new areas. Conservation Magazine published an article quoting research form one Peter A. Lindsey of Kenya's Mpala Research Centre who interviewed hunters who were travelling to Kenya. They found that 86% of them preferred hunting in areas where a portion of the proceeds went back into the local community and conservation efforts. They also found that they were willing to pay the same price for what they would regard as a poorer trophy if it was a problem animal that was going to have to be killed anyway. Nearly nine out of every ten were willing to hunt in areas that were poor for wildlife viewing or which lacked attractive scenery which offers a potential source of income to places that stand no chance of developing sustainable eco-tourism. But do keep in mind that these are simply the responses of the hunters themselves who I am guessing wish to show themselves in the best light possible. Whether they are actually behaving that way and whether hunting can be consistent with good conservation would surely require more research into its actual impact in the real world. According to a 2005 paper by Nigel Leader-Williams and his colleagues at the Journal of International Wildlife Law and Policy (which sounds like a riveting read!) the answer is that it might be. In South Africa they legalised the hunting of White Rhinos and as a result private landowners went out of their way to reintroduce the species to their lands so they could benefit from this new source of income. The population of White Rhino went from less than a hundred to over 11,000 at the same time as they were being hunted. Quite why the killing of these creatures could ever be viewed as 'fun' is beyond me and I'm unsure whether the hunters are mentally unbalanced in some way or just complete bastards, plus it hardly seems to demonstrate any skill on their behalf when they are hunting and tracking down their prey. How hard can it be to track an animal when from my experience most of them are content to wander up and stand next to the safari vehicles, you can just about reach out and touch them for god's sake. The problem is that while I feel that way I have never actually done anything to try to help these endangered species. Nothing real anyway, I might have dropped a few coins in a collection tin here or there and shaken my head in disgust at the stories in the newspapers but that's it. There are a lot of good people on the ground who are doing there best to protect these animals and who are willing to try different approaches to achieve it and in some places without the revenue from tourists they are thinking the unthinkable. I still think there must be something wrong with anyone who can derive pleasure from killing these beautiful creatures but I really can't judge those who view the hunters as a resource to be exploited for a benevolent end. It seems to me that until we in the West are willing to put our money where our mouth is and properly engage with the conservation work we are not in a position to pass moral judgements.

Next day at some ungodly hour of the morning we were awoken by a less than gentle knocking at the door. Mohammed had kindly arranged for the hotel porter to come and wake us so we could have an early morning game drive before breakfast. Having had somewhat less than half a bottle of wine (in spite of Shaun's insistence that he had poured it in equal measures) I felt quite fresh and ready for a day's safari-ing. We saw many more animals, nearer or further away than the ones we had already seen, we saw a lioness dragging a kill back to her cubs and Mohammed pointed out that there was also a vast diversity of bird species that could be seen here if only we could drag our attention away from the 'big game' animals for a few minutes including black kite, crowned crane, lovebird and sacred ibis, and then as we headed down another dirt track under another tree like so many others we spotted a large Eagle sat only a couple of feet above our vehicle. One of the German's (I really should have got their names) we were with got his camera ready and shouted at Mohammed that he wanted to take a picture of this, it would be a stunning shot from so close. We drove up and slowed down the Eagle unperturbed by our presence and as we drove underneath we came closer to the perfect spot for the shot,

"stop…. stop now" said our companion but we kept on going,

"Stop, Stop now, Stop" he said more urgently and still we kept going, the Eagle disappearing from view and the branches of the trees obscuring it more and more as we moved further and further forward,

"STOP, FUCKING STOP FOR FUCKS SAKE" he screamed, incandescent with rage, Shaun and I looked at each other and sank gently back into our seats realising that we were between him and Mohammed and both feeling that we would really rather not be. Shaun made brief eye contact with the man's wife who pulled a face that expressed surprise, shock, disbelief and embarrassment all at the same time. He couldn't get his shot of the eagle from here and as Mohammed tried to reverse back something spooked our feathered friend and he took off into the sky. There followed a period of acute embarrassment on all sides and a good deal of quite introspection but a few more sightings overcame that and after several more drives through the park we abruptly found ourselves back on the Mombasa-Nairobi highway and on our way back to the hotel. I had thoroughly enjoyed myself and seen some unforgettable sights but part of me was ready for some serious relaxation by the pool, the possibility of alcohol crossed my mind, possibly some snacks from the all-day bar. A smile on my face I settled back for the never-ending drive to the hotel.

The privation of the safari behind us we settled back into the comfort of the hotel finding a new appreciation for waiter service, drinks on tap and a comfy chair. Not travelling anymore was also appreciated just for now, not sitting in a hot leather seat with sweat sticking your clothes to you and having a pool to take a dip in as the whim took us was appreciated. We found ourselves meeting up with Peter and Margaret, our rummykub opponents of several days ago and played a few more games with a few more drinks and forming the very strong opinion that Margaret was a cheating bitch. That first day back we did nothing at all interesting which probably doesn't make very interesting reading for you so we had better move on to the next morning.

The sun was already well above the horizon and the temperature was rising fast when we finally dragged our arses out of bed. We had set no alarm and arranged no alarm call, relying on our bodies to decide how much sleep they would like. It turns out that it was quite a lot. We had missed breakfast and so we would have to see what was available from the pool bar. As we ate Shaun finished reading his copy of NOW magazine which had been purchased from the airport and on moving back to our places by the pool he dropped the magazine onto his sun lounger and wandered down into the pool, this seemed like a good idea so I followed him. As we swam around trying to cling to the small areas of shade at the edges Margaret came over to us and asked if she could borrow the magazine as she had finished her book and Shaun being a generous sort of guy said,

"of course, keep it, I'm done with it."

"thank you" she replied and wandered off

We finished our swim and got back out of the pool and I settled down to continue reading my book, the Agatha Christie murder mystery Curtain, the final Poirot mystery. I was about half-way through and the story had really got my interest so I was a little surprised when Shaun looked over, glanced at the cover and said,

"Is that the one where it turns out that ------ is the murderer?" (I've blanked it out so I don't spoil it for you)

I turned and looked at him, wide eyed with disbelief,

"why would you tell me that!"

"well, you've read it before haven't you"

"No"

"oh…"

This could have resulted in a serious squabble but we were interrupted by a man heading around the grounds of the hotel selling a motley collection of last week's English newspapers. Newspapers which he was attempting to sell at only ten times the usual asking price. In spite of the generosity of this offer we declined.

"well I do have this magazine as well."

Taking out a copy of NOW magazine.

"I don't normally get them but I have this one available."

Shaun looked at the magazine and then turned to me,

"that's a coincidence" he said innocently,

I just raised my eyebrows and this triggered some spark, his mouth forming an 'O' shape,

"she's traded it."

"yep."

"I only gave it to her a few minutes ago, she hasn't even read it, she has just traded it for a newspaper."

"yep."

"devious cow."

Our previous argument forgotten I tried to carry on reading with Shaun mumbling to himself about going over and giving her a piece of his mind which of course he didn't. The afternoon passed, the sun drifted lower in the sky, the waves lapped against the shore and I finished my book and then started a little more reading about the history of Kenya's independence. My view of Britain's dismantling of its Empire is somewhat sanitised as I think it is for most people. The idea in my head is that the 'wind of change' led to us voluntarily leaving behind our

Imperial aspirations and granting independence to all the former countries we had occupied. The truth in Kenya is a long way from this. The story of their struggle is a bloody and violent saga from which neither side emerges covered in glory. Beginning in 1945 a group of nationalists led by Kenyatta (their first President) had been pursuing purely political means to pressure the authorities into giving political rights and implementing land reforms to redistribute the valuable highlands to African owners. There efforts came to nothing and in the 1950's a violent insurrection began against British Rule. This was the Mau Mau rebellion, led mainly by the Kikuyu tribe who's economic interests had been marginalised for years by growing white settler expansion. By 1952 fighters from the Kikuyu, Embu and Meru tribes had begun attacking white settler farms and destroying livestock resulting in the deployment of British troops and a brutally fought counter insurgency that would last up until the 1960's. The number of people killed in the counter-insurgency operations was officially 11,000 with over a thousand of those hung by the administration, as against just 32 white settlers killed in the same eight years. The Kenya Human Rights Commission believes that around 90,000 were executed and over 150,000 detained in appalling conditions without trial. For a different perspective the professor of African Politics at Oxford University, David Anderson, has said that he believes the death toll to be around 25,000 which is bad enough.

> "Everything that could happen did happen. Allegations about beatings and violence were widespread. Basically, you could get away with murder. It was systematic."

He believes that the African Home Guard, which was organised by the British, controlled the population through oppressive violence.

> "The British armed the militia, rewarded them, incentivised them, allowing them to pillage property of the nationalists."

Leigh Day & Co, a London law firm, lodged a claim on behalf of five elderly Kenyans in 2009 alleging terrible treatment in detention camps by British-led soldiers. Solititor Martyn Day told the BBC:

> "They were put in camps where they were subject to severe torture, malnutrition, beatings. The women were sexually assaulted. Two of the men were castrated. The most severe gruesome torture you could imagine."

All this action on the ground was backed up by the R.A.F. who dropped over six million bombs on suspect targets between 1953 and 1955. The British response was total!

Leigh Day & Co represented over five thousand Kenyans and in 2013 the then Foreign Secretary, William Hague, expressed regret in the House of Commons for the atrocities and confirmed that the government would pay compensation and costs to all of the victims.

The violence and atrocities were not contained just to one side either. The Mau Mau themselves engaged in horrific acts. The raid on the loyalist village of Lari where the majority of the men were away fighting with the Home Guard is one such example, 70 mainly women and children were brutally massacred in one day. There were also many thousands of smaller attacks from single European women being stabbed to death in the streets to loyalist Tribal Chiefs being assassinated. The fact that after all of this we could emerge as allies, if not always agreeing on everything, is I think a remarkable testament to both sides. With all of this to mull over it was time to think about making a move and getting ready for the evenings activities.

Showered , dressed, suited and booted we headed down to the dining room on the way spotting a millipede crossing the path, jet black in colour and about twelve inches long, our cameras quickly came out for a few pictures, Shaun place his hand alongside it for one of the pictures so we could get a sense of perspective, without touching it of course as they secrete a noxious substance which can burn your skin. This kind of experience doesn't happen when your heading to dinner in Derby. We selected ourselves a table in the dining area, sat down, studied the menu and tried to catch the eye of a waiter to come and take our drink order. As the waiters bumbled around without ever getting close to us, not exactly avoiding us, just never seeming to move in our direction, Peter and Margaret wandered over and asked if they could join us.

"Certainly, you thieving cow" Shaun replied. Of course he didn't, what he actually said was,

"Of course, help yourself" but said with a tone that made it quite clear that her behaviour had been noted.

They had made a real effort for dinner and they did make us feel somewhat underdressed, except for the fact that Peter had reached the age where the waist of his trousers had begun getting higher and higher, virtually touching his nipples,

'they're nice trousers, what chest size are they?'

Is this the fate that awaits all men, once you pass retirement age something clicks in your head and you end up looking at trousers in M&S and asking assistants if they have anything that can be pulled up a little higher. A drinks order was placed and then after about 20 minutes and a couple more requests we went and fetched them for ourselves. We were offered a range of well-known brands at quite reasonable prices or we could drink the local stuff for free. We drank for free. Dinner passed without incident and the small talk filled up the gaps between courses. At one point Margaret enquired what was to be found in the fruit salad and I was reminded of a story about one of Shaun's Aunties who was offered an Orchard Salad and when she enquired as too its contents received the reply,

"Apples, strawberries, raspberries, mango, pineapple, cumquats and bananas."

"that's some fucking orchard!" she replied.

Trying not to laugh as I remembered her forthright response I asked what the orange dessert was. Apparently it was an orange with cinnamon,

"an orange what with cinnamon?" I enquired.

"just an orange."

If it hasn't got at least a thousand calories and enough cholesterol to drop a Moose then it has no place on a dessert menu in my opinion. I opted for a liquor coffee instead. At the end of the meal the waiter came over and let us know that there would be some entertainment out on the patio for us to enjoy. We headed outside to watch it as there was precious little else to do. We spent some time carefully selecting our seats, trying to make sure that we were close enough to see but far enough away to avoid any audience participation that might occur. There was no need to worry though as the entertainment was to be some traditional Kenyan dancing from a group of Maasai. I don't think any book that features this country would be complete without a mention for the Maasai, although the estimates have their numbers at somewhat less than a million much of my impression of the country is shaped by their culture. Their dress, homes, dancing and culture are recognised far beyond the borders of their own nation. Driven from much of their land, mainly by the British, they have retained their identity and semi-nomadic lifestyle even after many have moved into responsible positions in business and government. There have been some changes as the needs of conservation and the spread of the National Parks has infringed on the Maasai's livelihood, for example only a short while ago it would have been a matter of great pride for a young warrior to go out and kill a lion in revenge for the death of their livestock but a program has been rolled out, not fully accepted it has to be said, where they instead accept financial compensation for the loss of the animals in order not to deplete the lion population. There has also been the widespread practice of female circumcision which has drawn great criticism from inside and outside the country and although the practice is illegal and there has been an attempt to introduce a 'cutting with words' ceremony to replace it approximately a third of the population still practice the ritual. Change is happening but slowly. The clothing they wore was a long way from what I had expected as my expectations were for lots and lots of red. Admittedly I think that because of only a few programs on the telly back home and it is in fact quite wrong. The clothing is far more varied and multi-coloured with pinks, blues, oranges, browns, the whole spectrum in fact. They weren't just plain in design either but carried striped and checked patterns with flowery motifs against bright pink backgrounds. The warriors were able to pull off this look while simultaneously remaining quite menacing, you were in no doubt as to who the warriors were or the fact that they would be up for a fight.

The music and dance that we were to experience was typical of much Maasai music with a chorus of vocalists providing the harmonies and the melody sung by one or possibly several individuals known as the song leader or leaders. The songs follow a particular pattern, often a repeating pattern and are accompanied by a distinctive neck movement, they lean forward when breathing in and back when breathing out creating a rhythm of head movement that accompanies the song. We noticed that the males and females in the group never came into contact with each other during the dancing and singing even when there was a great deal of pelvic thrusting going on from both sides. The finale involved a jumping dance where the males took it in turns to jump as high as possible, repeatedly, without their heels ever touching the ground and singing in a higher pitched voice whilst doing this. This is a traditional dance that they were sharing with us and it was a lot more impressive than the Morris Dancers that a visitor to the U.K. would get to see. I do wonder if this traditional dancing has any real relevance to people in their everyday lives here or if it's just for show at certain times, is it for their benefit any longer or for the benefit of the tourists who are expecting to see something of the like. I realised how little time we would have to get to know the place and how we would only scratch the surface of this country and its people. I decided there and then that we would need to come back.

Some 5 years later we did attempt to go back but it was not a success. After a full day of travelling we arrived at our hotel and had only one day before being informed that a terrorist group had launched a number of attacks against the country and that we would need to be evacuated. There has been an ongoing struggle against Islamic extremism in Kenya, much of which is finding its way across the border from Somalia, but it escalated during our visit. The Foreign Office changed its travel advice to essential travel only and we found ourselves evacuated in convoy back to the airport and flown back home. I felt such sympathy with the staff at the hotel who found that an attack hundreds of miles away in the north of the country was going to see their livelihoods disappear. Tourists from all over the world were being evacuated as a result of the warnings and these people suddenly found themselves with an empty hotel and no source of income. It would be many months later before flights would resume and things could start getting back to normal. We were very angry at the time as it seemed an overreaction to the level of threat that we faced in Diani. We discovered later that the Foreign Office had in fact only issued warnings for the north of the country and in the city of Mombasa and the south of the country where we had been was unaffected. This resulted in a year-long battle with the travel company to get the cost of our holiday refunded along with our out of pocket expenses and which we only achieved on the eve of our appearance before the Independent Arbiter that had been appointed. I shan't name the company here but I am happy to state that they were absolute bastards who dragged their feet and obstructed us at every turn, they ought to be ashamed of themselves for behaving in such a shoddy way. Enough said, I had better get back to talking about the holiday that did work out.

We were woken one last time by the hotel reception and found that suddenly we had arrived at our last day here, only a few hours left until we would be heading to the airport. After packing our bags and checking the drawers for the sixth time (just in case we missed something the first five times) we thought that we should use these last few hours for something productive, a quick check of the activities board settled us on a visit to a snake farm. It wasn't so much a farm as a small yard with a number of hutches filled with different types of snakes. There were also a couple of large tortoises wandering around the floor and a large concrete pen in the corner with an Iguana in it. We were told that although the pen was open we should keep our hands well away if we valued having all of our fingers. The next two hours were a strange combination of interest and fear, a fascination with something new and the sensation of breaking into a cold sweat all mingled together. The hutches were not going to remain closed. We started off gently with some of the smaller lizards and they didn't pose too much of a problem for any of us. Once they were out of the way however we suddenly found ourselves face to face with the snakes. Our guide opened a hutch, reached inside and pulled out a writhing mass of small green snakes, all about 30cm in length and about the same width as an electrical cable. These were just a taster of what was too come but it seemed a good place to start so I held out my hands, cupped together and our guide dropped the writhing mass on to me. Surprisingly, as I have no experience of this, the snakes were not at all cold or slimy, their texture was rather unexpected and not as unpleasant as I had feared. Commenting to our guide about how docile they were he informed me that while that was generally true they could bite if they felt threatened or felt trapped or man handled

"But don't worry, they aren't venomous, the worst that can happen is you get a bacterial infection"

"Great." I said, not feeling particularly relieved.

"Don't worry, I have been bitten many times" he replied holding out his hand which was covered in numerous scars and was missing the ends of two fingers. He explained that as well as running this sanctuary to educate people he also provided a free service to remove snakes, including the more dangerous ones, from residential and tourist areas and then release them out in the countryside away from the human threat. I commented on the phrase 'human threat' and he informed us that snakes are very shy creatures who will go to great lengths in order to avoid contact with humans. We hunt them down, kill them, destroy their habitats, run over them, poison them and generally act to their detriment without thought and sometimes with deliberate malice, that is what this place was hoping to change. Each of his scars we were solemnly informed represented a step on the learning curve of his profession and we shouldn't worry as he knew what he was doing now. Feeling less than reassured we moved on to the next hutch and this is where it was going to get really interesting if a little less interactive. Before us lay a Cobra. Kenya has four species of these big beasts, the Black Necked Spitting Cobra, the Red Spitting Cobra, Egyptian Cobra and Forest Cobra. Their preferred haunt is under rocks, in thick undergrowth or in piles of dead vegetation. Catching these snakes is not easy as they are very aggressive especially when cornered and the spitting Cobras are deadly accurate in spraying their venom into your eyes from a respectable distance, this particular snake had apparently sprayed our guide and left him blind for nearly three days. He couldn't afford medical treatment so he relied on bed rest and washing his eyes out with milk until he got his sight back. I would have thought that anyone with any sense would use a grab stick and goggles but our guide seemed to think they were for amateurs. The one thing he did show us was a pair of shoes he used onto the bottom of which he had painted two eyes. Holding the sole of the shoe up to the snake means they strike at the shoe and not at him directly. He must have a hell of a lot of faith in his cobbler is all I can say. Should you be unlucky enough to receive a direct bite from a Cobra you can look forward to at least thirty minutes of paralysis until you pass away. We moved on to the next hutch and were shown a Python which is a constricting snake rather than venomous, it may still bite you but what you really need to worry about is it wrapping itself around you, if this happens then you are in deep shit. The Python here was only about 5 feet in length but that seemed to me to be quite long enough,

"So who wants to hold her?"

The group stepped back leaving a boy of about 11 stood out on his own at the front, he held out his hands and following the guides instructions to get a solid grip just behind its head and with the other hand to get a solid grip on its tail the snake was draped around his neck. These snakes grow very large and it is not uncommon to find nine-foot-long specimens out in the wild. These too like vegetation and rocks but they are more likely to be on top of them sunning themselves so at least there is less chance of stepping on them unexpectedly. Taking our turns with the snake and getting some nice photos the guide handed the snake to Shaun and said,

> "Make sure you get a good grip, she is going blind and is pissed off, you might only be a shadow but she can still aim for you if she decides to bite"

This led to a brilliant picture of Shaun wearing an expression that said he may shit his pants at any moment. The photo session over we moved on to the next hutch and the Puff Adder, considered to be about the most dangerous snake in Kenya, not only are they enormously venomous and quick to strike but they also enjoy lounging in clear areas where humans are likely to be wandering about. Should you disturb one there is at least a chance that you will get a warning. It will typically coil back into an 'S' shape and emit a loud hiss, you should not ignore this warning and believe me you do not want to find out why. Much to my horror these things apparently regard an unoccupied bed as an excellent place to curl up for a rest and there have been stories of people rolling over on them in the night and getting a nasty bite as a result. The penultimate hutch contained a boomslang, a tree dwelling snake, the males a bright green, the females a dull brown and that brings me onto a story about one Karl P. Schmidt, a herpetologist (snake expert) who worked at the Chicago Natural History Museum in the 1950's. Several of his colleagues had been unable to identify a green snake that had been presented to them and so they brought it along to Karl. Alas for him he worked out what it was shortly after it had bitten him and he realised that he was facing certain death as no anti-venom was kept in the United States for the Boomslang at that time. Ever the studious academic he chose to spend his final moments carefully documenting all the symptoms as they spread throughout his body, he kept writing until the moment he keeled over and passed away. Due to his thoroughness future generations of herpetologists would know about every agonising second of his death including the fact that he was bleeding out of almost every part of his body. The final hutch contained what is probably the most infamous snake in Kenya. The Mamba. This was a black mamba and the first thing that was easily noticeable was that it wasn't black, more of an olive green. The name black mamba stems from the colour of its mouth, when forced open its mouth is jet black, the green mambas mouth being green. One is deadly poisonous the other is not meaning that they all have to be approached with extreme caution. They can be over 10 feet in length and are very agile, able to turn back over their own body and strike behind them if captured by the tail. If they get you then it will all be over in about 20 minutes but the agony you will experience may make it seem a lot longer. As dangerous as they are their venom is being used in research to stimulate the growth of damaged nerves when amputated limbs are reattached in surgery. Every cloud as they say. These creatures are greatly misunderstood and we were told there is a lot of myth and urban legend surrounding them in the area. This guy on his own with very little help was trying to do his bit to educate people, to get past the primitive fear and appreciate what amazing creatures they really are. That said they can be incredibly dangerous and will quite happily try to kill and eat anything up to and including a Horse. They don't eat very often but when a snake is hungry it will set out to kill whatever is the first thing that it happens across and over the years they have been found to have swallowed some pretty amazing things from crocodiles and cows to electric blankets and light bulbs! The light bulbs along with golf balls can be mistaken for an egg which they see as a tasty meal but what the snake that ate an electric blanket was thinking I have no idea. There are even recorded instances of snakes eating themselves, they can become disorientated and strike at their own tail after which they manage to consume quite a lot of themselves before realising that something is not quite right.

One lesson that we learned again and again as we travelled around is that all these creatures from the snakes and the insects up to the elephants and the lions have so much more to fear from us than we do from them. If we

If we don't then we are going to end up destroying them and their habitats.

And that was it, our holiday in Kenya had come to an end. We have covered hundreds of miles, seen many animals in their natural habitat, met many new people and perhaps learned a thing or too. We had made a few holiday friendships, you know the sort, get on great for a week or two, exchange a couple of e-mails when you get back and then never hear from each other ever again. Our bags are packed, our paperwork is in order and all that's left is too sit around in reception waiting for the coach, sit around on the coach waiting to get to the airport and waiting around at the airport for the plane to take us home.

One last thing, if you have enjoyed reading this book could I ask you to log on to Amazon and leave me a review! 5 stars would be great and will help me sell some more books to pay for more holidays. Cheers.

Printed in Great Britain
by Amazon